"This book is full of fascinating in[formation about love and] attachment. It uses the newest data fr[om] molecular biology to explain how we l[ove and] how to develop this deep human capacity by understanding oxytocin. I learned a lot about myself and the people I love."

> —Helen Fisher, professor at Rutgers University and author of *Why We Love*

"*The Chemistry of Connection* is a beautiful book about how to nurture lasting love between ourselves, our mates, and our children. Kuchinskas gives readers essential information about connection and bonding. She helps readers understand the brain chemistry behind who we are."

> —Michael Gurian, author of *The Wonder of Girls* and *What Could He Be Thinking?*

"*The Chemistry of Connection* is a marvelous book. It brings the science of oxytocin into the service of love in an engaging and practical way. Anyone who wants to understand and improve his or her relationships should read it."

> —Paul J. Zak, Ph.D., professor and director of the Center for Neuroeconomic Studies at Claremont Graduate University, discoverer of the relationship between oxytocin and trust

"We know intuitively that hugging and cuddling are not just good for you, but essential ingredients to well-being. This book explains why. Read it to learn how to get more nurturing connection in your life."

> —Reid Mihalko and Marcia Baczynski, creators of Cuddle Party

"In *The Chemistry of Connection*, Susan Kuchinskas helps her readers understand important aspects of how oxytocin enhances relationships, and more importantly, how to navigate some of the obstacles we encounter on the often rocky road to love."

> —Barton Goldsmith, Ph.D., author of *Emotional Fitness for Couples* and *Emotional Fitness for Intimacy*

the chemistry of
connection

How the Oxytocin
Response Can Help You
Find Trust, Intimacy,
and Love

SUSAN KUCHINSKAS

New Harbinger Publications, Inc.

Publisher's Note

Distributed in Canada by Raincoast Books

Copyright © 2009 by Susan Kuchinskas
New Harbinger Publications, Inc.
5674 Shattuck Avenue
Oakland, CA 94609
www.newharbinger.com

Cover design by Amy Shoup; Text design by Amy Shoup
and Michele Waters-Kermes; Acquired by Melissa Kirk; Edited by Nelda Street

---

Library of Congress Cataloging-in-Publication Data

Kuchinskas, Susan.
 The chemistry of connection : how the oxytocin response can help you find trust, intimacy, and love / Susan Kuchinskas.
     p. cm.
Includes bibliographical references.
ISBN-13: 978-1-57224-623-2 (pbk. : alk. paper)
ISBN-10: 1-57224-623-5 (pbk. : alk. paper)
1. Oxytocin--Popular works. I. Title.
QP572.O9K83 2009
615'.782--dc22

                                        2008052315

Mixed Sources
Product group from well-managed
forests and other controlled sources
Cert no. SW-COC-002283
www.fsc.org
© 1996 Forest Stewardship Council

11   10   09

10   9   8   7   6   5   4   3   2   1

First printing

contents

acknowledgments

Sue Carter was extremely generous with her time and information, sharing her papers, patiently explaining her work, and offering rigorous comments on the oxytocin craze. Karen Bales was my first guide to the fascinating neurochemistry of bonding. Paul Zak kindly shared his groundbreaking work with humans, as well as his encouragement and friendship. Peter Gray's early enthusiasm and comments provided an impetus to keep going, while his fascinating research on fathers greatly added to this book. My editors, Melissa Kirk and Jess Beebe, believed in this book, and offered deep and thoughtful comments throughout the writing process. My agent, Jeff Kleinman, was invaluable in helping me shape the work. The dogs I've shared my life with, Benson, Amaryllis, Toby, and Udupi, taught me to nurture. Hypnotherapist Marilyn Gordon helped me to fire my work with a pink glow. Linda Jean Cranmer ushered me into the amazing world of birth and opened me to a rebirth of my own self. Joe Picard and Chico State University allowed me to enjoy two days with Allan Schore, the guru of attachment, during the Children in Trauma conference. My soul sisters, Linda Donahoo, Jessie West, and Janis Mara, provided a secure base from which I could explore and challenge myself. In addition, Jessie's tender and tough editing was a big help in getting my story straight. My parents, William and Gloria Kuchinskas, have always done everything they could for me, and still do. My sister, Margi Lee, is a mirror, a foil, and a pal. My niece Kate has brought much healing to my family, and let me experience baby love for the first time. And last but not least, Mike Freeman is the love of my life. Thank you, sweetie, for everything.

introduction

The Inuit don't really have twenty-eight words for snow (despite popular belief), but we humans could use twenty-eight different words for love—in any language. We employ this single inadequate term, "love," to describe a multitude of states, from the way a stranger's touch sends fire across our skin to the crazed period when we can't stand to be away from our lover to the delight we feel in our grandchildren.

This book talks about one kind of love: the deep, enduring bond of committed love, the kind of bond forged by oxytocin. Oxytocin floods our bodies with feelings of connection, trust, and contentment. This neurochemical is released during orgasm, creating that lovely afterglow. It travels through the bloodstream as it rouses the pleasure center of the brain when we're stroked, when we're physically close with loved ones, and even when we share time with close friends. Oxytocin is the secret to forming committed relationships, turning lust into long-lasting love. The oxytocin bond is the basis for lifelong relationships of all kinds: between parent and child, two siblings, or even two close friends. Oxytocin lets you live happily with a life partner. It keeps you up all night with a colicky baby. It makes you glad to donate a kidney to your sister.

It may seem unbelievable that love, one of the most complex and intense experiences of life, could depend on a single chemical. And, in fact, oxytocin doesn't make its magic in a vacuum. Human biology being the incredibly complex system that it is, oxytocin cooperates with several other neurochemicals to make it feel good to be with friends and lovers, to make it feel better than almost anything else. It interacts with the neurochemicals of pleasure to make sex and love rewarding. It stimulates the release of prolactin, the hormone that readies the female body and brain for childbirth and mothering.

We humans are hardwired for love and connection. Because of the way our brains respond to the mix of oxytocin and dopamine, humans are among the estimated 3 percent of mammals that are monogamous (Insel 1997). Now, biologists define monogamy a bit differently from the way we think of it in the context of marriage. They see monogamy not as about sexual exclusivity but, rather, as a way of life. *Socially monogamous* animals live together in stable family units consisting of a mated pair and their offspring. Males and females cooperate in gathering food and caring for their young. They do mate for life, although both mates may occasionally copulate outside the pair.

The difference between a socially monogamous animal and a promiscuous one seems to be the way oxytocin receptors—the cellular structures that take in specific molecules—are distributed. Monogamous mammals have more oxytocin receptors in the parts of the brain that handle social interactions and reward. Because of this, the monogamous mammal not only remembers the pleasure of sex and interaction but also ties that memory to his or her partner.

But oxytocin isn't just about sex. In 2004, Andreas Bartels and Semir Zeki, of the Max Planck Institute in Germany, scanned the brains of men and women as they thought about their beloveds, and then scanned the brains of mothers as they thought about their babies. They saw the same parts of the brain become active in these different emotional states, parts that are rich with oxytocin. Anytime you look at bonding, any kind of bonding, you find oxytocin. Dogs enjoy a burst when someone pets them, guys given a snort in the lab suddenly trust each other, and couples resolve spats after a whiff.

While oxytocin lets us remember whom we love, and makes it rewarding to be with them, it does much more than create feelings of attachment. It's active throughout the body, relieving stress and promoting healing. As oxytocin flows through the bloodstream, it lowers blood pressure, reduces cortisol levels, and improves digestion (Uvnäs Moberg 2003). That's why love not only makes us happy but also keeps us healthy.

So, if our brains are wired for love and our health demands it, shouldn't we move toward emotional and physical intimacy—of all kinds, not just sex—as simply and naturally as a flower turns toward the sun? If our brains are made for love, why do we need online dating and divorce courts? Why is it so hard to find and keep love? Why do we feel so alone?

It's because loving isn't automatic. We learn the oxytocin response— that is, we learn to love—after birth, from our mothers. A baby's brain completes its development outside the womb, in the first three years of life, and this development is shaped by interactions with the mother. That's an immense task for one person, and it's astonishing that most accomplish it so well. Such a powerful relationship has the power to do harm instead of good. During this critical period, many things can inhibit or twist what should be a natural response to physical intimacy. Trauma, abuse, or neglect can impair the brain's ability to use oxytocin, locking it into a perpetual fear state. If the oxytocin response doesn't develop in a healthy way, you may fall in love without loving. You may marry without loving. You may die without ever loving and being loved.

But the brain isn't made of stone. It's living flesh that continues to grow and change all our lives. Because of this *neural plasticity*, new circuits and new ways of responding can continually develop. Just as you can learn to play the piano or make guacamole no matter how old you are, you can learn how to love—even late in life. Understanding the oxytocin response can not only help you understand why you feel the way you do, but also help you learn to feel the way you want to, so you can form the kind of attachments you crave. When you understand the basis of love, you can begin to consciously retrain the oxytocin response.

This book gathers together research in psychology, neuroscience, and molecular biology carried out with human and animal subjects, and then takes a leap into possibility: an explanation of how we love, why we sometimes can't, and how we can learn to love at any age.

Chapter 1

making the connection

for some of us, love is elusive and strange. We may quickly fall into what seems like a deep connection with someone, but it dies as quickly as it flashed into being. We may choose partners who are cruel or indifferent, and thus never get the comfort and love we so desperately need. Friendships wither or explode in anger and misunderstanding. Sometimes we feel wrapped in a thick blanket of isolation that affection can't penetrate.

There are many ways love can go wrong but only one way it can go right. The secret to the deep and lasting connection we think of as true love is in *oxytocin*, the brain chemical that lets us bond, trust, and mate. The brain normally releases oxytocin, sometimes called "the cuddle hormone," when we're physically or emotionally intimate with someone. Quite simply, this brain chemical is responsible for making us feel loved and secure. It may seem unbelievable that love and commitment to a mate, one of the most complex and intense experiences of life, could depend on a single hormone. Why haven't we heard of this before? Where can we get some?

The Connection Chemical

Oxytocin was the first hormone to be identified, when, in 1909, Henry Dale discovered that an extract of pituitary gland caused uterine contractions. He derived the name "oxytocin" from the Greek for "quick birth," and later found that oxytocin also contracted the muscles around mammary glands, causing the milk letdown phenomenon. For many years, scientists thought oxytocin's role was limited to childbirth and breastfeeding. They had no clue that it also affects our emotions. Kerstin Uvnäs Moberg, the Swedish scientist who identified the connection between oxytocin and love, dubbed the oxytocin response the "calm and connection system" because of its dual action on the body and the mind (Uvnäs Moberg 2003).

Not Just for Pregnancy

Many women find breastfeeding to be a deeply absorbing, meditative experience. The world seems to drop away as a mother gazes down at her baby. She's wrapped in a profound peace, and may feel an oceanic joy and cosmic connection, not only with the infant but also with everything else. Uvnäs Moberg first realized the calming power of oxytocin when she nursed her own children. In her book, *The Oxytocin Factor*, she writes: "In pregnancy, nursing, and close contact with my children, I experienced a state diametrically opposed to the stress I was familiar with in connection with life's other challenges. I was aware that the psychophysiological conditions associated with pregnancy and nursing fostered something entirely different from challenge, competition, and performance" (Uvnäs Moberg 2003, xiii–xiv).

Intrigued, Uvnäs Moberg began experimenting with rats, administering oxytocin to see what happened. The rats were calmer, and their blood pressure and cortisol levels went down. After several treatments, the rats became sleek and healthy. Their immune systems were tuned up, and wounds healed faster.

Uvnäs Moberg then began a long collaboration with a group of midwives, testing oxytocin levels in pregnant and nursing women, checking their blood pressure and other physiological responses, and asking them about their feelings. She saw that women with higher levels of oxytocin in their bloodstreams were calmer, less anxious, and more attentive to their babies. Over time, it became clear to her that oxytocin isn't just for nursing mothers; it's vital for everybody and for every facet of life, from love to digestion to wound healing.

The Chemical Cocktail

Oxytocin doesn't do its work of bonding us to one another all by itself. Your brain is bathed in a complex cocktail of chemicals that controls its myriad functions. *Neurotransmitters* are substances in the brain that carry messages and trigger responses. They can also influence how responsive brain cells are to various ingredients in the chemical cocktail. Candace Pert, the biologist who discovered how cells take up opiates, calls the neurochemicals that create emotional states the "molecules of emotion" (1997).

These molecules of emotion include *serotonin*, which is important for regulating moods; *norepinephrine*, a molecule of excitement; *dopamine*, the molecule of attention and reward; and, interestingly, *estrogen* and *testosterone*. We think of estrogen and testosterone as hormones that control the reproductive system, but they also play a major role in regulating processes in the brain, including mood and emotion. Now, we know that oxytocin also plays a critical part in regulating many daily bodily processes, and as I'll show in this book, it's crucial for emotional bonding in both men and women.

ebb and flow

The balance of chemicals in the brain's emotional cocktail constantly shifts, as does the cells' sensitivity to them. When the amount of serotonin available to brain cells dips, we feel blue. When we get a jolt of dopamine in the brain's reward center, it feels powerfully pleasurable. And, when oxytocin floods the brain's trust and connection circuits, we feel a range of emotions from trust to deep love.

Our bodies undergo a similar ebb and flow of these molecules of emotion, triggered by what's happening in the brain. This is the mind-body connection at work: The brain takes in information from

7

the senses, processes it, and—unconsciously, in less than a heartbeat—"decides" how to react. It then sends a jolt of chemical messages through the bloodstream, mobilizing the body to react.

A Question of Balance

Life is made up of cycles: sleep and waking, work and rest, stress and relaxation. To respond to life's shifting demands, your body uses two parallel structures: the *sympathetic* and *parasympathetic* nervous systems. These two systems of nerves extend throughout the body, working together to keep us in balance, neither overaroused nor apathetic, as we deal with the events of the day. When you need to be alert and active, the relevant brain circuits light up and send chemical messages to the sympathetic nervous system. When it's time to kick back, have fun, or get well, the parasympathetic nervous system takes charge.

We know a lot about the sympathetic nervous system, the body's accelerator. Maybe you know your heart rate and blood pressure, or have had your cortisol level checked. High blood pressure and high cortisol levels are signs that the sympathetic nervous system is overactive. Simply put, you're stressed out. But we're only beginning to understand the parasympathetic nervous system—and how important it is for health and well-being. If cortisol is the marker for an activated sympathetic nervous response, oxytocin is the sign that relaxation has begun. Oxytocin is the antistress chemical.

It's too bad so little attention has been paid to the role of oxytocin in chilling out the stress response. This omission has blinded us to an important truth about being human. Because oxytocin is also the chemical of love and connection, when we have love and affection in our lives, we tend not to be chronically stressed (Bale et al. 2001; Cacioppo et al. 2006). Love not only makes us happy; it makes us healthy too. By means of oxytocin, love heals.

The HPA Axis

The sympathetic nervous system has nothing to do with the phenomenon we call sympathy. Rather, it commands our survival reflexes, mobilizing the body to flee from danger, to fight when we need to. It galvanizes us to go after a reward, using cortisol, adrenaline, noradrenaline, and vasopressin to deliver its fight-or-flight messages. We spend our days in a state of slight arousal, the sympathetic nervous system prepared to respond to stress in a heartbeat. When danger looms, the body goes on alert. Whether it's a mugger, a manager, or someone competing for a parking space, our bodies react just as they did when a lion prowled over the hill.

The body's stress response circuit is known as the *HPA axis*. Its command center is the *hypothalamus*, a part of the brain that manufactures many of the molecules of emotion. The hypothalamus ties in to the *pituitary gland*, a chemical storehouse, and the *adrenal glands*, which produce adrenaline. Stress is such an insidious malady, because we react to it unconsciously. And we react to opportunities for love, the antistress feeling, just as unconsciously.

The HPA axis is part of the *limbic system*, a part of the brain where activity takes place below the level of conscious thought. It's closely tied to the *amygdala*, the part of the limbic system that's thought to be directly responsible for emotional reactions, how we feel about the input coming in through our senses. The amygdala integrates information from the senses, particularly vision, and makes snap decisions on whether something the body encounters is interesting, delightful, or dangerous. When the eyes see an angry face, the amygdala tells the body to get out of there. When they see a hot cookie—of the human or confectionery kind—the amygdala places the body on a different kind of alert, preparing to seize the prize. In addition, the amygdala helps assign emotional value to what the senses perceive. The amygdala of the person scarred by a dog bite processes the sight of a canine and calls it dangerous; the amygdala of a person who grew up with a dog as a best friend assigns excitement and pleasure to the same sight. The amygdala makes similar friend-or-foe judgments about people (Adolphs, Tranel, and Damasio 1998). When the amygdala identifies a foe, it stimulates the HPA axis to release cortisol.

After the amygdala processes sensory information, it sends that signal up to the cerebral cortex, the thinking part of the brain, for further analysis. But it can also prompt action on its own and, in emotional situations, often does so, without waiting for thought or judgment from the higher faculties.

The HPA axis is like a muscle: the more you use it, the stronger it gets. But this is not such a good thing. An infant whose HPA axis is continually overstimulated will become a tweaked-out adult. Chronically elevated cortisol levels can damage the heart, cause high blood pressure, suppress the immune system, and make you susceptible to type 2 diabetes. That's why you need to chill when you're stressed out.

The Chill Factor

If you think of the HPA axis as your inner warrior, the parasympathetic nervous system is the peacemaker—and its dominant chemical is oxytocin. A body stuck in fight-or-flight mode will wear itself out. So, even as it tweaks the sympathetic reflexes, stress of any kind also stimulates the parasympathetic nervous system to release oxytocin, putting the brakes on the stress response.

The hypothalamus is not only the hub of the HPA axis but also the switchboard for the oxytocin loop. It produces oxytocin and releases it directly into the central nervous system. It also sends oxytocin to the pituitary gland, which stores it and releases it into the bloodstream in response to stimuli. The end point for the oxytocin system is receptors located in the brain and throughout the body.

Oxytocin receptors are cellular structures that can bind with molecules of oxytocin and draw them inside the cell, where they can be used. Receptors and hormones are like locks and keys; any receptor can only bind with a single chemical. A molecule of cortisol will sail right past an oxytocin receptor, while a molecule of oxytocin will latch onto it.

When the danger is past—or you've parked the car—the parasympathetic nervous system eases your body back from fight and flight, allowing you to rest and repair. It slows the metabolism, breathing, and heart rate, as it increases blood flow to the digestive system and activates the salivary and digestive glands.

While the sympathetic nervous system is dominant during the day, in the evening when you're safe at home, the parasympathetic system begins to predominate, digesting the evening meal and preparing for the night's sleep.

Friend or Foe?

In the past few years, brain-scan studies have begun to confirm Uvnäs Moberg's theories as they map oxytocin's cooling effects. Oxytocin is not only the body's radiator coolant but also the human race's social lubricant.

While there are oxytocin receptors all over the body (Gimpl and Fahrenholz 2001), the ones that produce feelings of love and connection are located in the parts of the brain that handle interpersonal relationships. These brain circuits are sometimes known as the "social brain." Oxytocin makes the social brain circuits come alive (Insel 1997).

A technology called *functional magnetic resonance imaging*, or *fMRI*, lets scientists observe which parts of a person's brain become active when he or she performs different tasks. For example, when researchers at Justus-Liebig University in Germany used fMRI to watch men's brains as they looked at pictures of threatening or fearful faces, they found that a whiff of oxytocin not only calmed the activity of the amygdala but also cut down the signals it sent to the brain stem, the so-called "reptilian brain" that acts without conscious thought. The oxytocin kept the men from responding to the hostile images with anger or aggression, as the control group did (Kirsch et al. 2005).

The hypothalamus pumps oxytocin into the brain when we have sex—and it floods the body and brain at orgasm. A hug or any loving touch can produce a spurt, earning oxytocin its nickname. When oxytocin reaches the brain's social center, it interacts with other feel-good chemicals to make us relate the warm-and-fuzzy feeling to that particular person, creating the bond we call love, whether it's maternal behavior, a marriage, a child's attachment to his mother, or the trust we place in a friend. That's why it can be so soothing, so delightful, to kiss, cuddle, and canoodle.

However, while our biochemical plumbing supports the deep bonds of love and friendship, we're not born with a developed oxytocin response: we're not born ready to love. We have to learn how.

Why Newborns Can't Love

Human babies are only half-baked when they emerge from the womb. The offspring of no other mammal is so weak, so undeveloped, so helpless for so long. Not only is the human brain not fully formed at birth, but also the sophisticated chemical factory that stimulates and controls how it grows is not up to speed.

In 1800, peasants captured a strange boy in the woods of France. This "feral child" seemed scarcely human. About twelve years old, he'd survived alone in the woods for years. He couldn't speak, preferred to be outside even in bitter cold, and relieved himself like a non-housebroken dog.

He eventually landed in the care of Jean-Marc-Gaspard Itard, a Parisian physician who tried to socialize him, with limited success. The boy became world famous as Victor, the Savage of Aveyron, but died at age forty without having learned to communicate (Shattuck 1980). If you could have put Victor under a modern fMRI scanner, his brain would have looked very different from the brain of a child raised from birth by Dr. Itard or any other family of that era.

Shaping the Brain After Birth

Every newborn is like Victor, a wild brain waiting to be trained and civilized. While each of us is born with unique genetic codes determining how our brains will develop, the extent to which those genes are activated depends on experiences after birth. The external events that activate, deactivate, or modify the activity of genes are known as *epigenetic*. The development of oxytocin receptors and their sensitivity appears to be greatly influenced by epigenetic factors.

Certainly, some neural systems are immediately online: we emerge from the womb knowing how to breathe, how to swallow, and how to open our eyes. But the infant body must learn other vital processes in the first few months of its life: the ability to regulate the body's temperature, to maintain a steady heartbeat, and to calm down and stop crying.

The kinds of mothering the baby receives can create new neural connections or strengthen existing ones. Mothering also trains that baby brain to release oxytocin in times of safety and comfort. In response to loving care, the neural network (Moberg's calm and connection system) begins to branch out. How many oxytocin receptors the baby brain develops, how sensitive they are, and how much oxytocin is produced depends a great deal on how much nurturing, love, and intimacy the baby gets in the first few months of life.

Mothering

A few words about the notion of "Mother" are in order here. While her father and other people who care for her will eventually begin to influence the way her brain grows, during the first year, a baby's brain is shaped mostly by her mother. It's as though the still-incomplete infant brain can't grasp more the one "Other." That Other is usually the woman who gave birth to her, but it doesn't have to be. To a baby, the essence of mother is the one person who holds her close. When they talk about infant development, psychologists use the term "primary caregiver," acknowledging that today's families don't fit a single model.

Anyone can provide mothering: a single dad, one of a gay couple, an adoptive parent, an older sibling, or a nanny. Mother, then, can be seen as a role rather than a biological state, and mothering is the sum of all the nurturing and care an infant receives from the person she's closest to. I'll continue to use the simpler term, "mother." But remember that mothering is a relationship and that anyone can play this role.

Temperament definitely plays a part. Some babies come out of the womb shy or very sensitive. Their threshold for fear may be lower, their senses more acute. This basic temperament influences the way a baby responds to what he sees, hears, tastes, and feels. Still, whether his predilections are reinforced or reduced depends on his experiences after birth. The anxious baby can be soothed, and if he is, his brain may respond less anxiously to the next loud noise (Schore 2007).

The oxytocin response should begin to form in the first few months, and continue to develop through the first three years. But it won't happen automatically. It seems that mothering—the right kind of loving attention—is what sparks the genetic potential for a brain rich in oxytocin into realization. Being nursed, cuddled, and cooed over by his mother stimulates the growth and directs the pattern of oxytocin receptors in the infant brain's reward center. If he doesn't get much attention, the parts of his brain designed to handle social interactions won't develop the complex interconnections that make those responses strong and healthy. There will be fewer oxytocin receptors there, and they may not be as sensitive to oxytocin.

Licking, Nuzzling, and Loving

Animal studies illustrate this shaping process. It's especially clear in rats, those laboratory stalwarts. A good mother rat spends a lot of time licking and grooming her pups; this is her primary nurturing behavior, aside from actual nursing. But not all females are equally demonstrative. Some mothers lick a lot, some just a little.

In Michael Meaney's lab at McGill University (Champagne et al. 2001), researchers have found that how much "love" a baby rat gets— how often its mother nurses it, how long she spends nuzzling its wriggly little body and grooming its downy fur—influences how many oxytocin receptors develop in its brain and how sensitive they are. Baby rats that get plenty of attention from their mothers are highly sensitive to oxytocin—and they grow up to be mellower. It's harder to get them stressed out, and when they do become anxious, their stress response isn't as strong. When the females grow up and mate, they give the same kind of attention to their own babies.

Karen Bales (2007), a psychologist at the University of California at Davis, specializes in tracking how early experiences can shape a life, and she's found a strong connection between mother love and the ability to bond later with a mate. In her work with prairie voles, she's found that the smallest change to how a pup is handled can create lifelong differences in its behavior.

The prairie vole is a roly-poly little creature, about four inches long, with a big head and short tail. It builds a system of runways both underground and on the surface, rearing one or two litters of pups each year in a nest made of dry grass. These pups grow up fast; they reach adulthood within thirty days, becoming ready to mate and breed their own litters. Juveniles live with the family group until they mature enough to mate. When a single male finds an available female, he stays close until she comes into heat. Then they copulate as many as fifty times in a couple of days. After that sexual marathon, they settle down together to raise little voles. Males and females mate for life, spending much of their free time cuddling—or "huddling," as biologists say—with each other and their offspring.

The male is highly involved in caring for the babies. He's a great father, minding the pups while she goes foraging, and retrieving them when they wander away from the family huddle. This happy family life continues until death. Because prairie voles are such a social animal, they're a superb species for studying social behavior.

In the laboratory, prairie vole families are housed in clear plastic bins about the size of a shoe box, with a floor of wood shavings and cotton for nesting. They typically get moved to a clean plastic cage once every week or two. Lab assistants wearing gloves simply pick them up by the scruff of the neck and plop them into the clean container. Babies remain attached to their mother with sharp milk teeth so that when the mother is lifted, they fly through the air attached to her teats. Following this startling treatment, the mother voles carefully inspect their babies, and then give them an extra session of licking and grooming.

Bales experimented with reducing the handling the voles received by scooping some of them up in a plastic cup, while treating the others as usual. Three rounds of this treatment produced differences in the pups' social behavior when they matured. The female voles whose mothers had received normal handling by the lab assistants grew up to form monogamous bonds when they mated, a characteristic of this species. The females whose mothers hadn't been handled couldn't form a pair-bond, while the untouched males were less interested in caring for their offspring. All the voles in the group that was handled less were generally warier than the handled group.

How do you tell whether two voles are bonded to each other? They'll show a preference to be with each other rather than with other voles. Jessie Williams, a University of Illinois zoologist, developed a standard test for partner preference (Williams, Catania, and Carter 1992). You place one vole in the center of a three-part cage. In one of the side sections, you tether its mate; in the third section, you tether an unfamiliar animal. The vole in the center can move freely between the two others, so you keep track of how much time it spends in each section of the cage. More time spent with either vole than alone in the center shows that it wants social contact; more time spent with the mate shows that it prefers that animal to the other.

Normal male voles are so strongly paternal that they'll begin to take care of any pup that's around, whether or not it's their own. To see whether there was a difference in the parental instincts between the handled and unhandled males, Bales introduced each male to a pup it had never seen before, then kept track of how much time it spent in behaviors such as huddling next to it or bringing it back if it wandered, as well as any aggressive moves. The unhandled males were much less likely to retrieve or huddle with the pups. Like Meaney, Bales believes that the differences in the adult voles' bonding and parenting are due to the babies in the handled group getting increased attention from their mothers following the disturbance of being moved. Being moved likely recreates periods of danger that would naturally occur in the wild. The mothers react by going into grooming mode, which probably stimulates the oxytocin response in both mother and pups (Bales 2007).

Learning to Love Love

So it's not that babies need an absence of stress or fear. Instead, mothering teaches them how to cool themselves down after stressful or frightening experiences. At the same time, babies learn that other people are reliable sources of soothing and connection. Once oxytocin receptors have begun to spread throughout the infant brain, oxytocin interacts with other brain chemicals to make bonding—love—one of the best sensations around.

Mommy's loving touch releases endorphins that stimulate the brain's reward centers, while dopamine activates both the reward system and social memory. Oxytocin plus endorphins and dopamine create the intensely pleasurable bond that will be the model for all the baby's future relationships. At the same time she's learning the oxytocin response, her infant brain is being trained by these interactions to associate mother—another person—with comfort and care.

If she's lucky, she learns to feel deep comfort and joy when she's close to Mama. She begins to associate the good feelings of touch and and nourishment with that particular person among all the others who hold her, touch her, and coo at her. Later, this same combination of oxytocin and reward will allow her to bond with family, friends, and, eventually, a mate and children.

A well-developed oxytocin response will guide her, as well, through other kinds of relationships. The oxytocin system will come alive in any kind of trusting interaction, for example, in business or a cooperative endeavor. And the combination of dopamine and oxytocin will make it feel good to be generous and help others (Moll et al. 2006).

But while our biochemical plumbing supports the deep bonds of love and friendship, we're not born with a developed oxytocin response: we're not ready to love. We have to learn how. What happens to you in the first three years of life, especially the kind of nurturing you get, shapes your oxytocin response—the way you love—for the rest of your life.

The Chemical Code

Oxytocin isn't the only brain chemical involved in emotion. All our emotions—all the flavors of anger, anxiety, and happiness—are the result of chemical responses that have evolved over aeons to exquisite precision. The nervous system is composed of neurons: nerve cells that communicate with each other via chemicals known as neurotransmitters. Neurons pass along electrical impulses. When these reach their destinations, they trigger releases of chemicals that create changes in the body in response.

Different brain systems take charge of various functions and emotions, and they employ different sets of chemicals to control cellular processes. Each sensory event triggers a cascade of chemicals in the brain that informs the nervous system and prompts it to react.

Oxytocin: Crucial for maternal behavior, it also bonds lovers to each other and parents to their children. It reduces anxiety, allowing for relaxation, growth, and healing.

Vasopressin: Similar in chemical structure to oxytocin, it's central to male bonding, and motivates men to defend the family. In men especially, it may increase anxiety or put the body on alert.

Dopamine: A motivating neurotransmitter that's key to the brain's reward system, it combines with oxytocin to tie the pleasure of orgasm to a specific partner.

Serotonin: A natural antidepressant and mood elevator, serotonin levels rise when we fall in love, and fall when we're depressed.

Estrogen: This sex hormone increases the bonding effects of oxytocin in women.

Testosterone: The sex hormone that fuels sexual desire in men and women, it also diminishes the bonding effects of oxytocin in men while increasing the vigilance and protectiveness effects of vasopressin.

Prolactin: This hormone stimulates maternal behavior, especially in nursing mothers; it also produces sexual satiety in men and women.

Epinephrine (or adrenaline): A hormone produced by the adrenal glands, it raises blood pressure, increases the heart rate, and makes us breathe faster, preparing us to respond to danger or stress.

Norepinephrine (or noradrenaline): Central to the brain's emergency response, activating the fight-or-flight system in extreme situations, it puts the body on alert in exciting or interesting situations.

Cortisol: The adrenal glands secrete cortisol in times of stress to protect the body; levels of cortisol rise in the throes of romantic love.

Your Oxytocin Boost Checklist

In the rest of this book, you'll learn much more about how and when our brains release oxytocin. Get started experiencing the benefits right now with these simple activities:

- ☐ Offer a sweet kiss.

- ☐ Share a warm hug.

- ☐ Cuddle.

- ☐ Make love.

- ☐ Have an orgasm (alone or with someone else).

- ☐ Sing in a choir.

- ☐ Give someone a neck rub.

- ☐ Hold a baby.

- ☐ Stroke a dog or cat.

- ☐ Perform a generous act.

- ☐ Pray.

- ☐ Root for your team.

Chapter 2

how babies learn to love

humans evolved as social animals. Our brains are designed to navigate through the shifting demands of love, friendship, trust, and affiliation. Our bodies demand the flush of oxytocin that comes with positive social interactions. The release of oxytocin in a baby's brain as he's nursed, cuddled, and cooed over by his mother stimulates the growth of oxytocin receptors in his brain's reward center that will later allow him to bond with friends and, eventually, a lover. But each of us goes through an individual period of evolution that begins in the womb and lasts for the first three years of life (Schore 2003). How we evolve—and, most important, how our oxytocin system evolves in response to mothering—will determine how we connect with others throughout our lives.

How Mothering Shapes the Oxytocin System

For a baby, life is very simple: "I'm frightened, so I'll cry." "I'm being held; I can stop crying." But underneath that simple behavior is a superbly orchestrated series of neurochemical events taking place in systems evolved to ensure the baby's survival. The baby's fear activates her HPA axis, releasing cortisol into her system, causing her to cry. Her crying activates her mother's own HPA axis, sending Mommy into alert that something's wrong with the baby. As Mommy picks her up and rocks her, the baby calms as her hypothalamus releases oxytocin. At the same time, oxytocin cools the mother's sympathetic nervous system, replacing anxiety with a feeling of sweet connection. These chemical events become a habit that we begin to learn only after birth.

In the first three years of life, the brain goes through a huge growth spurt, nearly tripling in size and forging billions of connections between neurons. *Neural scripts*, habitual patterns of emotional response, begin to develop (Schore 2007). The simple interaction of crying and soothing is one example of a neural script. Because the baby's cries were answered and she was comforted, the progression from fear to cries to calm becomes a familiar scenario, expressed in the brain as a series of chemical cascades. Later in her life, a tone of voice or facial expression may trigger this same cascade.

At the same time, a use-it-or-lose-it process called *neural pruning* begins: while the parts of the brain that get more use become stronger, neurons that aren't used wither away. A child's early experiences help determine what connects to what, which parts of the brain are more active, and how her brain reacts to internal and external events. For example, a baby born into a household that loves music may develop a stronger sense of rhythm and a finer ability to detect changes in tone than one born into a less musical family. This pruning process also seems to take place with nerve cells that should be organized into brain circuits for attachment. Without secure emotional attachments and enough loving touch, the brain may never develop the ability to love (Perry 2002).

The Emotional Thermostat

Soon, under Mama's care, the baby will gain some control over his own physiological functions and also over his emotional states. Psychologists call the ability to maintain an even emotional keel *self-regulation.*

Self-regulation is similar to the rather moralistic concept of self-control. But it's not about stifling feelings or repressing desires. It's the process whereby the conscious mind soothes the instinctive fears, rages, and lusts of the amygdala, while choosing to respond to events in ways that will most likely achieve its goals. For example, the baby screams for attention, but a ten-year-old realizes that screaming for something he wants in the supermarket will only get him into trouble. So, he instead calms his frustration, and uses his "inside voice" to negotiate. This process is known as *down-regulation.*

Another aspect of self-regulation is what psychologists call *up-regulation:* opening up to excitement, joy, delight, and love. Without this ability, life isn't as much fun. The goal of self-regulation is to be able to experience life's highs and lows to their fullest without "losing it" (Siegel 1999, 246–47).

Healthy affect regulation lets us respond appropriately to what's going on around us. It uses a variety of conscious and unconscious techniques to influence feeling and, at its most basic, our biochemistry. When you psych yourself up before a speech by running around the block, you're revving up your fight-or-flight system to become highly alert and focused. When you take a deep breath before you respond to your spouse's angry words, you're practicing affect regulation. That long breath signals your amygdala that it's not time to fight, while it wakes up the parasympathetic nervous system.

The bag of tricks for self-regulation isn't necessarily internal; the ability to reach out to others for help is part of a healthy individual's repertoire. When you say, "I need a hug," you're craving affectionate touch to activate the oxytocin system in order to calm down and relax. Grabbing the phone to share the excitement about your promotion is a way of savoring the triumph; calling a friend to say hi when you're feeling lonely invites her to soothe your blues away. The ability to engage in this kind of affect regulation—a little help from your friends—depends on a well-developed oxytocin response. If a child has learned that being with other people feels good, she'll automatically seek out situations where she can experience an oxytocin release.

Moms Make Hotheads Too

Mothering also determines how strong our stress response is. We all know people who are hotheaded. What they really have is a hot amygdala. The newborn limbic system is ripe for the soothing effects of oxytocin. But it's equally vulnerable to anxiety, fear, and depression.

A baby will inevitably have some not-so-sweet experiences. The discomfort of a wet diaper, the shock of a loud noise, and even a couple of minutes when Mama is away making lunch can seem like abandonment. Danger—and, for a baby, forty-five seconds away from Mama can feel life threatening—activates fight-or-flight reactions in the HPA axis that can become limbic habits, part of an individual's collection of neural scripts. When he feels terror at being separated from his mother, his HPA axis shoots cortisol and adrenaline through his bloodstream. His baby brain instinctively puts his body into a state of high alert, because when his ancestors found themselves in this situation, it often meant death. Today, it may mean merely that Mama needed to get a drink of water or make a phone call. But his genetic origin as a creature of the wild still shoots fear chemicals through his brain.

When he's picked up and comforted, his pituitary gland releases oxytocin, which soothes the jangle of cortisol. In time, his brain learns that being apart from his mother is not the life-or-death situation it was for his monkey forebears. His sympathetic nervous system doesn't become as highly aroused, because his brain expects that crying will soon be rewarded with comfort. As long as he's got someone to kiss away the tears, this will become part of his emotional lesson: there will be fear, and fear will be followed by comfort and connection. This is how he learns to trust his mother and, eventually, other people. The cycle of fear and then comfort, expressed in his physiology as adrenaline and cortisol followed by oxytocin and dopamine, is another example of a neural script.

In the months of holding, rocking, cuddling, nursing, and baby talk, Mama's soothing touch will set the pattern for the down-regulation of fear—if that touch comes. We can guess that, if not enough sweet nurturing takes place, or the baby experiences too much stress or fear, oxytocin receptors may wither and die, leaving the developing brain with less ability to take up oxytocin—and to feel loving and loved (Bales et al. 2007a).

Anxiety Threshold

While an infant's distress can sear the memory system of the right brain with a deep impression, usually the sensitivity of the HPA axis develops over time, shaped by many events and interactions with the mother. But horrific events, such as abuse or grave injury, can push the fragile infant limbic system into permanent overdrive.

Edward Tronick, an associate professor of pediatrics and psychiatry at Children's Hospital Boston who studies how exposure to violence and trauma affects children, has proposed an explanation of how a baby's brain could get stuck in a permanent state of fear, known as *hypervigilance* (Tronick 2002). His theory also explains how a mother teaches her baby to regulate his own internal state.

According to Tronick, in the course of the day, a baby cycles regularly through different states in which he's more receptive to different kinds of emotional input. Simply, he's in a certain mood. During one part of this cycle, for example, he may be more open to positive interactions. If his mother smiles at him or tickles him, he'll react with joy—and fall into that mood state. After the first positive stimulation, it will take less to trigger his pleasure the next time. If there's no smile or love to be had, on the other hand, this particular opportunity for happiness will pass him by. But if he's not in the part of his mood cycle where he's open to cheer, all the tickling in the world won't make him smile. It's the same with negative emotions. When he's in a cranky state, a sudden noise or jostle can put him in a bad mood, while the same jostle when he's in a happy mood won't bother him a bit.

Tronick suggests that the more intense the emotional input the baby receives and the longer it lasts, the deeper and longer the baby will sink into whatever mood it provokes. A grouchy mother will, over time, increase the duration of the baby's susceptibility to crabby moods, make it more likely he'll fall into them, and make it harder for him to move out of them.

To illustrate this, let's take a look at two babies and their mothers.

*Darrel wakes up in the morning in a neutral state. His
sympathetic nervous system sends just enough cortisol into
his system to wake him up and make him alert for the day.
Mama comes to him, takes him into her arms, and cradles him
against her heart. This sweet input is enough to push him over
the threshold into a positive mood state, as dopamine begins to
stimulate the reward center of his brain and oxytocin sends his
body into relaxation. As he's fed, the good feelings and oxytocin
intensify. Because the release of oxytocin in the brain has a
feedback effect, if he gets more love from Mama he'll be even
more likely to release oxytocin and to stay in a happy mood.*

*As this interaction repeats itself every morning, Darrel learns
to expect that he'll be taken care of. But one morning, Mama
gets up early and decides to grab a quick shower before the baby
wakes up. Darrel finds himself alone. He feels distress, and his
HPA axis is activated. However, because his sensitivity to positive
interactions is heightened and his sensitivity to negative ones has
been lowered, his stress response is mild.*

*Of course, if Mama doesn't come, he'll become more and
more anxious, until he's in a full-blown fear state. This negative
mood won't pass easily.*

*But Mama does come. As soon as she shuts off the shower,
she hears Darrel's cries, throws on her bathrobe, and hurries
in, her hair dripping wet. She holds Darrel and comforts him,
initiating the expected cycle of soothing and intimacy. The
oxytocin flows.*

*Darrel soon comes to associate other people with the good
feelings of oxytocin. Even milder social interactions will stimulate
his oxytocin response, and he'll view the world as a source of
positive interactions.*

Let's watch another baby as he starts his morning.

*Tyler, too, wakes up in a neutral mood, but his mother doesn't
come to him right away. Time is tight for her in the morning. Her
two-month maternity leave went all too fast; now she's back to*

her nine-to-five schedule. This means she needs to get the baby and his three-year-old sister to day care by 8:20. Her husband has already left for his forty-five-minute commute.

Tyler doesn't know this; all he knows is that Mommy isn't there. His ancient survival instincts kick in. He's alone, and that means he's in danger. He starts to cry.

Now, Mommy comes to him, but she's not happy about the crying. Her touch is loving, but her voice is exasperated. "Can't you ever give me a break?" she asks him.

He's now in a full-blown negative mood state, with elevated cortisol levels. "Uh oh," says the day care worker on Tyler's arrival. She gives him a cuddle, but when he won't be soothed, she puts him down to let him cry it out.

The next day isn't any better for Mommy or for Tyler, nor is the next one. As the week goes on, it takes less and less negative stimulation for him to fall into a bad mood. His HPA axis is turned up, and his oxytocin response is turned down. Soon, Tyler's nervous system expects fear and distress when he wakes up. His amygdala becomes more active in order to deal with this daily state of perceived threat.

On Sunday, Mommy is more relaxed, and she's determined to give Tyler a really good morning. While Daddy cuddles his sister, she takes the baby to bed with her. Gazing lovingly into his eyes, she croons to him, reassuring him that he's her adorable baby boy.

But Tyler's system has gotten used to morning stress. Her touch does elicit the oxytocin response in him, but it's a muted response and not enough to counteract the weeklong routine of anxiety. He stays in his anxious mood. Mommy is disappointed. "I just can't make him happy," she tells people.

Next Sunday, she doesn't expect Tyler to enjoy a cuddle, so she doesn't put much effort into it. Tyler is even less able to respond to her unenthusiastic attempts, and a pattern is set. "Tyler doesn't really like to be held."

When Tyler grows up, his bad moods are disconnected from actual events. He wakes up angry. He completely misses friendly overtures from coworkers, because his brain has learned to expect indifference and annoyance. Someone would practically have *to throw her arms around his neck and say over and over, "I like you," to get his attention. His emotional dial tone—and its underlying neurochemistry—has been set.*

As Tronick says, these chronic bad moods aren't something that a baby will grow out of; instead, he grows into them. Tyler will be more prone to anger or depression throughout his life, and less open to joy.

Both these mothers acted as co-regulators of their babies' internal states: the emotions they expressed when they interacted with their babies combined with the babies' internal predilections to cocreate the babies' moods. On the neurochemical level, the mother's actions influenced her baby's release of cortisol or oxytocin, even as the baby's behavior influenced the mother's internal state. This process of two people's internal states becoming aligned is known as *limbic resonance.* In its positive form, it can be one of the deepest pleasures we know.

The Attachment Gap

An ad for a business credit card shows a man seated at his desk in a home office. His left hand is on the keyboard, as his right clutches the mouse. Propped up on his forearms is a baby, holding a bottle to her mouth with both hands. The man is hunched over, peering at the monitor. His hands and eyes connect to the computer, not to the baby. She stares into the distance.

The credit-card company wanted to show that it understood its customers' busy lives with the photo and a caption about how doing business requires multitasking. The ad also illustrates a recipe for attachment problems and a scenario that's becoming all too common.

What's this multitasking father communicating to his baby girl? He isn't engaging in that dance of rising and falling emotion that leads her brain through states of arousal and calm. He's not stroking her body to show her how sustenance comes from touch. The message he's sending her is, "Your physical needs will be met, but caring for you is just another project I need to get done."

In this hyper world, it's all too easy for a parent to be distracted during feeding, severing the connection at its most sensitive moments. It's so hard to slow down and just sit there while the baby suckles. It's so easy to chat on the cell phone with a baby in your lap, and it makes the time pass quicker. But your gabfest is an affront to the baby's whole system at a time when she needs peace and quiet. Babies suffer not only from inattention; but also their sensitive nervous systems and delicate physiological responses take a bruising from our always "on" lifestyle.

If Mommy smokes as she holds her baby, he may develop an aversion to physical contact. If she's nervous or uncertain as she cradles him, he'll learn to feel anxious when another draws near. If she's harsh or abusive, he'll grow up to view the world as a hostile realm filled with people with whom he must fight for survival.

Distracted feeding can hinder the development of the baby's oxytocin response, but it can be bad for parents too. When you relegate feeding and holding to the array of tasks you must complete to get through the day, you deprive yourself of your own oxytocin boost. Settling down with your baby calms your HPA axis and improves your ability to cope with stress throughout the day. Even more important, this quiet time reinforces the bond between you and your child.

We don't automatically love our children the minute they appear out of the womb. Everything from a difficult birth to labor-room anesthesia to a weak oxytocin response in the parents can reduce the oxytocin surges that normally accompany birth and spark mother-love. In a 1980 study of first-time mothers, 40 percent said their predominant emotional reaction when first holding their babies was one of indifference. This take-him-or-leave-him feeling could have been due to exhaustion from a difficult birth; it also could have been the result of the drug-induced fog in which many women labor. Indifferent mothers in this study were more likely to have had their membranes ruptured artificially, endured a painful labor, or taken a dose of Demerol (Klaus and Kennell 1983, 37).

Some parents feel guilty or worried if their first reaction to the newborn isn't "enough." They shouldn't. Everyone's different, and this physiological response isn't necessarily automatic. Still, there's probably no more powerful an oxytocin producer than a baby (Champagne et al. 2004). Many people who've struggled with grown-up relationships understand love for the first time when they have a child. The bond will grow every time you hold your baby and look into his eyes—as long as you pay attention and let it happen. It's not always easy to carve out that time. But if you don't, there's a danger that you may not achieve the deep bond that will support your relationship with your child as you move through the challenging years from toddler to teen.

Mothering and Oxytocin Styles

Long before brain-imaging technology was developed, and before oxytocin's role in forging bonds began to be understood, psychologists realized that we don't all learn to love the same way. In work spanning the 1960s to the 1980s, psychologists John Bowlby and Mary Ainsworth identified three different *attachment styles* that describe a child's bond with his mother (Bowlby 1990). These attachment styles can be seen as reflections of how someone's oxytocin system has developed. In fact, in light of today's understanding of neuroscience, you could call them "oxytocin styles."

Ainsworth developed a protocol known as the "Strange Situation" to determine how a baby or toddler was attached to his mother. She carefully scripted eight short episodes that briefly place the child in situations that could be stressful or frightening. The Strange Situations are designed to uncover the implicit terms of the relationship between mother and child.

To begin the twenty-minute Strange Situation test, the mother and baby are brought into a waiting room. Behind a one-way mirror, researchers watch. After mom and baby are settled, a researcher enters and approaches the baby, taking the lead from the baby's reaction. If the baby is distrustful or frightened, the researcher backs off. If the baby is interested or accepts this unfamiliar presence calmly, the psychologist may engage him with eye contact and smiles.

Next, the mother goes out, leaving the child alone with the researcher. After a few minutes, she returns and comforts her child; then the researcher departs. Mommy soon follows, leaving the child alone for a little bit. The researcher comes back, soon followed by the mother. Finally, mother and child are left alone for a final reunion.

How these separations and reunions go is a good indication of how the child experiences his relationship with his mother.

Secure Attachment

A *secure* infant will happily explore the toys in the room, without being unduly wary of the stranger. He may cry when his mother leaves, and then run to her when she comes back, easily consoled and contented in her arms again. He knows he can always count on his mother to quickly come to him and care for him. His oxytocin response is strong and immediate.

Avoidant Attachment

But some babies seem unconcerned when Mommy leaves, nor do they worry about the stranger in the room. An *avoidant* child greets her return with indifference or even resists being picked up. He doesn't depend on mother's attention and love; in fact, he's resigned himself to getting along without it. Maybe he's been left to cry for hours; maybe circumstances like a hospital stay have caused too long a separation. He's learned to protect himself from disappointment or rejection by trying not to need Mommy. His oxytocin response may be weak, or he may have found ways to self-soothe by evoking oxytocin without the need for another person.

Anxious Attachment

A third group may be clingy when Mom is present, extremely distressed when she leaves, and angry when she returns. Such a child is never sure whether Mommy will come back to him or of what's going to happen when she does. As a result, he's confused and miserable. Ainsworth dubbed this the *anxious* style of attachment. Mommy's care may have come with a dose of anger or resentment, or she may have been sweet sometimes and distracted at other times. As a result, this baby's oxytocin response may be inappropriate. For example, his brain may not release oxytocin unless anger or rejection is part of the interaction.

The Emotional Set Point

Whatever style a child's relationship with Mommy takes, according to attachment theory, that becomes a "set point" for intimacy. As an adult, he will unconsciously take whatever steps he must to make sure his relationships follow that pattern. A friend who genuinely admires him seems creepy to an avoidant person. An anxious person may drive friends and lovers away with his incessant demands for reassurance, while he rejects people who love him unconditionally.

You may see yourself in one of these descriptions, or you may already have been aware that you don't feel secure in relationships. But knowing this doesn't seem to make a difference, because these patterns are remarkably resistant to change. A toddler can't be expected to understand the subtleties of relationships, but even a grown-up who solves physics equations and makes a perfect soufflé can be just as baffled by them. That's because a lag in the development of the two hemispheres of the brain makes it nearly impossible to understand the emotional responses we learned from Mommy and Daddy.

The Divided Brain

In addition to the different brain circuits we've talked about, there's another division that's important for understanding our emotional lives. The brain is divided into two hemispheres, and each handles different mental processes. The left hemisphere is the rational side; the right hemisphere is the emotional side. That period of individual evolution that shapes the brain after birth begins with the right hemisphere; the left hemisphere doesn't become fully functional until around the age of three.

the emotional side

The right hemisphere absorbs a baby's first lessons about life. This is the place where those neural scripts, the conditioned emotional responses she learns, are stored (Schore 2007). It also handles *implicit information*: the emotional tone of an event rather than the details.

Throughout her life, it will be dominant for emotional processing and social interactions.

When you're deep in conversation, staring into someone's eyes, so in sync, your right hemisphere is fully engaged. Your tone of voice matches your friend's, and your body language might mirror hers. You immediately understand what she means. You respond without hesitation or conscious intention, because your right hemisphere has taken in and processed all the sensory and emotional information she's expressing without words. In turn, you react to this implicit information unconsciously, although, of course, you may at the same time be aware of what you're both feeling.

The right hemisphere is also more densely connected to the autonomic nervous system than is the left hemisphere. It's dominant for regulating the sympathetic nervous system and the fight-or-flight response, as well as the oxytocin response. That's why emotions shake our bodies so much more than our thoughts do.

The brain circuits that identify safety and danger, that produce feelings of attachment and the basic sense of self are formed in the right hemisphere during the preverbal and preconscious period. These unconscious assumptions, based on our primal experiences, influence the minute-by-minute conscious decisions the cerebral cortex—the thinking brain—makes; they also trigger the unconscious production of the neurotransmitters and modulators that produce your basic emotional dial tone and the signals the rest of the body sends to the cortex.

Even before birth, the right hemisphere gets busy learning to decipher social cues. Its ability to get attention and care from Mommy will determine whether the baby survives and thrives. The vocabulary of the right hemisphere isn't words but faces, tones of voice, and gestures. This half of the brain is superb at discerning subtle nuances of expression or tones of voice and responding appropriately. When you just "know" what someone's thinking, that's the right hemisphere in action.

the rational side

The left hemisphere handles language. It lets us name and describe things; it stores *explicit memories*, those movie-like images of things we've seen and done. And it's the side of the brain that makes sense of events. A day or two after that intense conversation with your friend, your left hemisphere may bring up the memory of your talk. You see again the way your friend's eyes close in pleasure or the mischievous way she giggled. You think, "She's really happy with her new job." The left hemisphere has examined and analyzed your interaction, and named the emotions that were involved.

However, the neural wiring in this hemisphere doesn't really take off for the first three years. This lag in development of the left hemisphere is why kids typically show a surge in their ability to talk at age three. It also explains why everything that happens before then, in that preverbal period, remains, for the most part, indescribable and inaccessible to cognitive processing by the left hemisphere (Schore 2003).

By the time the left hemisphere—the rational, analytical half of the brain—gets up to speed and we become self-aware, the brain structures that determine how we see the world and, most important, whether we see others as sources of love and contentment are already formed. For example, a toddler can have a wonderful time at the zoo with the grandfather she knows and adores, but have no conscious memory of the trip when she's older. Nevertheless, the smell of cotton candy might trigger a feeling of ineffable delight, while she recognizes Grandfather as a reliable source of affection and pleasure.

In other words, your emotional life—your capacity for human connection—is controlled by autonomic responses learned willy-nilly and unconsciously (Cozolino 2002, 12). By the end of the first three years of life, you'll develop the basic strategies you'll use to navigate the emotional complexities of adulthood. Romance and marriage, parenting, competition at work, negotiating with friends and enemies to get what you want—you'll handle these tasks with the neural scripts you developed before kindergarten.

How Mothers Learn to Mother

It's clear that mother love is the origin of all love. But if mothering shapes the baby's brain, what shapes mothering? Evidently, the same process that builds the infant's oxytocin system also forms the adult's parenting responses.

Remember how, among Meaney's lab rats, there were devoted mothers and careless ones? This behavior isn't inherited; it's based on how much oxytocin-producing nurturance the mothers received when they themselves were babies.

To determine whether "nature" or "nurture" made the female rats eager or apathetic mothers, Meaney and his colleague, Frances Champagne, cross-fostered pups. In 2004, they placed litters birthed by attentive mothers in the cages of indifferent mothers and gave the young of inattentive females to the attentive mothers (Champagne et al. 2004).

Both batches of pups grew up to be like their foster mothers. Those who'd been licked a lot spent plenty of time grooming their own babies, even though their genetic heritage was that of a careless mother. The rats born of attentive mothers but raised by neglectful ones neglected their own young.

The rats who behaved more maternally had more oxytocin receptors in their brains—and extra estrogen during pregnancy increased the sensitivity of these oxytocin receptors, causing them to take up even more oxytocin. The females who groomed their babies less had fewer oxytocin receptors in the brain, and an extra dose of estrogen didn't make them more sensitive to oxytocin.

These researchers found another clue to the way their rats mothered. The more maternal mother rats—those who spent more time nursing, licking, and grooming their babies—were more responsive to dopamine's effects in the *nucleus accumbens*, an important part of the brain's reward-seeking circuitry. The less-attentive mothers also reacted less to the motivating effects of dopamine in the brain's reward center.

Somehow, all that licking and nuzzling changes the way a baby rat's brain reacts to oxytocin, for good.

In rodents, the brain's reward system fires up when they nurse their pups, and in human mothers, all it takes is looking at their children to deliver a neural reward.

Remodeling Mama's Brain

If you've ever wondered how new mothers find the courage to undertake the task of keeping a mysterious and delicate newborn alive, or looked at your own children with a bit of awe that you made it through the perilous first few months, oxytocin is the answer. A mother has to fall in love with her baby before she can teach him how to love in return (Hrdy 1999).

Without oxytocin to lull them and dopamine to inspire them, too many new mothers might give in to the temptation to leave their red, squalling babies on the side of a mountain and move on.

In fact, a newborn baby may be the most powerful motivator there is (Champagne et al. 2004). Everything about taking care of her baby, including the spit-up and dirty diapers, becomes exquisitely pleasurable, due to a supercharge to the brain's reward system that's part of a remodeling process the female brain undergoes during pregnancy.

Pregnancy not only acts on the mammary glands and uterus, preparing the mother's body for labor and birth, but also makes the mother a little smarter and a lot more loving. As her body prepares to physically nourish the baby, her brain primes itself to adore him—and to teach him to love her back (Insel 1997).

Estrogen, progesterone, and prolactin, the hormones of pregnancy, enlarge the neurons in the hypothalamus, the brain's oxytocin factory. The bulked-up hypothalamus pumps out more oxytocin, while oxytocin receptors proliferate in the brain and become more sensitive (Bealer et al. 2006).

Dopamine is another part of the home brew that intoxicates a mother with love for her baby. Dopamine acts like a motivator in the nucleus accumbens, the brain's reward center. It fires us up to go after a prize, be it food, sex, love, or a baby's survival.

A Rush of Love

These effects aren't due to a permanent increase in the overall level of oxytocin in the "mommy brain," however. Instead, what seems to strike the bond is a spike in whatever the normal level is.

In 2007, in the first study of women's oxytocin levels over the course of pregnancy, childbirth, and nursing, Ari Levine, Orna Zagoory-Sharon, Ruth Feldman, and Aron Weller of Bar-Ilan University in Israel tested the blood of sixty-two mothers-to-be. They wanted to see if there was a correlation between the women's oxytocin levels and their bonds with their gestating babies.

They checked oxytocin levels in the first and third trimesters of pregnancy, and again one month after delivery. They also had the women answer questionnaires designed to show how attached they felt to this developing life inside them.

They found two surprising things: first, not everyone showed the same pattern of oxytocin levels. One third of the women maintained consistent levels throughout their pregnancies; the levels of another third rose about 40 percent from the first to the second trimester. The third group's levels dropped about 30 percent in that period. There were similar differences in levels from the second to the third trimester.

The second surprise was that it wasn't the women with the highest oxytocin levels who felt the most bonded; it was the women whose oxytocin *increased* the most from the first trimester to early in the third trimester.

This finding mirrors an earlier study of women who'd given birth at the Karolinska University Hospital in Stockholm. Kerstin Uvnäs Moberg measured levels of oxytocin in the new mothers' blood and correlated those with physiological indicators of stress, such as higher blood pressure, as well as with the women's own reports of how they were feeling (Uvnäs Moberg et al. 1990).

Moms with the strongest *pulses* of oxytocin while nursing were also the calmest. They had less need for stimulation or variety. Instead, they craved peace, quiet, and hours alone with their babies. At the same time, they became more open to others who were already close to them; visits from family and friends became more important and more satisfying (Uvnäs Moberg 2003).

thinking about pregnancy

Pregnancy creates a complex emotional state. There's wonder and awe at the way a new being grows from a single cell. There's excitement and also anxiety about an immense change in a woman's life. There's courage to muster to meet the challenge of caring for this precious new baby. And there's dread that something may go wrong.

So, in a parallel study led by Ruth Feldman (2007), the Bar Ilan team also looked at what these mothers-to-be *thought* about their babies. They asked the women to speak about their hopes and fears for the new lives they carried. After the women in the Israeli study had their babies, they returned to the lab for one more round of tests. Again, the women filled out questionnaires designed to uncover both protective thoughts, such as worry about the baby's health, and pleasurable ones, such as imagining how it was to hold the infant after she was born, as well as how often she actually checked on the baby.

They also videotaped the mothers interacting with their three-month-old babies to see how much each of them engaged in typical mothering behavior: gazing down into the baby's face, speaking baby talk, and affectionately touching and stroking the little one.

The scientists found that, among these natural emotions, oxytocin was tied to both the pleasurable aspects of a mother's love and her concern for her baby's well-being. The mothers with higher levels of oxytocin checked their babies more often, had more positive thoughts about their babies, and engaged more in sweet maternal behaviors.

This study suggests that oxytocin may not only prime the mother for those instinctive loving looks and gentle touches but also for the mental processes she'll need. Oxytocin will remind her to check on her baby, to constantly keep him in mind. And it will make all this feel wonderful.

While these studies provide more evidence that human love has the same hormonal basis as the bond a mother vole feels for her pups, they also illustrate another aspect of love that may be unique to humans: that fat cortex, the thinking brain, allows us to make complex mental representations of the world and the people in it.

Colic Connection

A Turkish study gives a fascinating glimpse into the way mothering styles get passed down in humans from generation to generation.

Researchers at the Marmara University Medical School in Istanbul hoped to solve the mystery of colic. Colic isn't really an illness, despite the feverish screams and milky spit-up that make these middle-of-the-night episodes terrifying for frazzled parents. It's defined simply as uncontrollable crying bouts lasting longer than three hours at a time and happening more than three days a week (Akman et al. 2006).

About 20 percent of babies get colic, usually in the first four months of life. It's an indiscriminate ailment, affecting boys and girls, firstborn and later born, with equal punishment. Doctors don't know what causes colic, and there's no cure. All they can recommend is experimenting. Remedies usually start with diet. Breastfeeding mothers are urged to avoid eating things that might make their milk taste different, such as cabbage or coffee; bottle-feeding moms are told to try switching the formula.

Ipek Akman, a pediatrician and member of the Marmara medical school faculty, wondered whether there might be something more fundamental at the root of colic, specifically, if there might be a relationship between a mother's mood and the baby's upset. He and his colleagues tested seventy-eight mothers of newborns for symptoms of depression and anxiety; they also gave the mothers a written test to determine whether her attachment style was secure or insecure. Akman's theory was that colic might be associated with either a mother's mood disorder or her inability to form a secure bond with her child.

The researchers found colic in seventeen of the babies, or 21.7 percent, which was right in line with estimates of its prevalence in the general population. But they found that mothers of colicky babies had significantly higher symptoms of depression. And 62.5 percent of the mothers with colicky babies had insecure attachment styles; among the lucky mothers without constantly screaming babies, only 31.1 percent had an insecure attachment style. The results were strong enough for Akman to conclude that both symptoms of postpartum depression and insecure attachment styles are associated with infantile colic.

If we look at Akman's study in light of what we know about oxytocin, it's easy to imagine the sad cycle that takes place. An insecure mom finds it hard to open up to her baby; she doesn't assume that he'll love her. She spends a little less time cuddling and cooing—or maybe a lot less time than the baby needs.

The baby hasn't learned how to soothe himself. The cortisol level of his blood rises; he's anxious, so he cries to alert his mother that he needs help. But his crying makes her anxious, and she feels more depressed at seeing her baby unhappy. The baby reacts to her own anxiety by becoming more upset, but she sees him as rejecting her attempts to comfort him. She must be a bad mother, she thinks. Now, she's more anxious and depressed. The baby, attuned to her biochemistry and mood, feels worse and cries harder. Soon, they've established the pattern doctors call colic.

Interestingly, many of the measures recommended to soothe a colicky baby are also good ways to short-circuit this negative feedback loop by creating an immediate connection between mother and baby. Carrying him in a sling or backpack places the baby's body against his mother's, where his immature parasympathetic nervous system can pick up the mature rhythm of the parent's. Tummy rubs, back rubs, or a warm shower in Dad's arms focus parent and child on their connection, creating soothing pulses of oxytocin.

Colic is only one small example of the way that a strong bond with Mother and a deep sense of security affect a baby's health and well-being. It's not surprising that children who are securely attached to their parents grow up to be secure young adults, but we may underestimate just how much that secure base gives them an advantage in every aspect of life.

A healthy oxytocin response helps children perform better in school, have more positive attitudes about work, and feel more confident about their ability to choose a career (Larose, Bernier, and Tarabulsy 2005; Bernier et al. 2004; Mikulincer and Shaver 2007). A weak oxytocin response, on the other hand, can keep a child from obtaining the help and support he needs to thrive (Cacioppo and Hawkley 2005).

The Circle Widens

By the end of the three-year period of rapid brain evolution, a child's emotional thermostat—how she reacts to stress and intimacy—will have been set. A healthy oxytocin response will set her emotions to a nice, even temperature, so she'll be neither hotheaded nor fearful. Oxytocin will foster the healthy development of the prefrontal cortex, the seat of judgment and rationality, giving her the ability to think before she acts and to curb her impulses when necessary.

A secure relationship with Mommy stimulates the oxytocin response in a healthy way—and a healthy oxytocin response creates a virtuous circle. As she cuddles with Daddy or tumbles around with her brothers and sisters, more oxytocin is released, making her still more gregarious. There's pleasure to be found in all kinds of relationships.

As a child's circle widens from Mommy's breast to Daddy, and then to family, friends, and strangers, her brain will apply the oxytocin pattern she learned as an infant to her extending circles of intimacy.

There's even evidence (Schore 2007) that how well her immune system develops—how strong it will be, how well it will be able to combat disease and environmental stressors—is determined by the kind of care and the depth of the attachment the baby has with her mother.

Children with oxytocin-rich blood are curious and eager to make friends. When they encounter strangers and new situations, they're less afraid, more confident, and able to connect quickly. They're able to develop empathy and behave altruistically. They're also more emotionally resilient; they can handle stress and rein in destructive impulses. The ability to connect with others while controlling their emotions appropriately gives them advantages that will last their lifetimes.

My Parents' Child

Not everyone finds it easy to reach out to others for comfort and support. Not everyone's a "people" person; some of us are remarkably self-contained, painfully shy, or downright misanthropic. These individual differences are partly the result of biological temperament and partly the result of how mothering and other early experiences have shaped the oxytocin system.

Scientists think that the way the brain continues to grow after birth enabled humans to be smarter; if the brain reached its full size and potential in the womb, the baby's head would be too big to pass through the birth canal. There are also adaptive advantages to letting postnatal experience help shape the brain.

It's important for a child to have a sense of belonging within his family. The more his temperament is like his parents', and the closer his emotional thermostat matches his parents' settings, the easier it will be for them all to get along. As long as his primary interactions are with his parents, the child who craves just as much, or as little, intimacy as his parents feel comfortable giving will fit well into the family dynamic.

If he enjoyed secure relationships with his mom, he'll tend to reach out to whomever he meets, seeking to draw them a little closer. It just feels good to him to be close. He knows in his body that the best place for another person is in the circle of his arms. When two secure people meet, the oxytocin flows freely, and they naturally draw together and build a relationship. They're the people who marry early, who can't wait to start their own families.

If his parents were anxious or avoidant, the same attachment style that enabled him to get along with them can keep him from forming healthier connections when he grows up. A weak oxytocin response may make him seem cold and distant to others, while he feels edgy or nervous in social situations. If he had an angry mommy, he'll freak when that oxytocin feeling begins to trickle through his veins. He'll date women who like to keep their distance, or angry ones who'll help him recreate the rage-filled home he's used to.

The woman who, as a baby, tried every trick she could to entice her mother but never got the sense of security she craved will find that her own emotional thermostat reflects that dynamic. Close will never be close enough. She'll be so hungry for attention and affirmation that no one could ever satisfy her. Her raw need will scare away even the most loving people.

Let's look at the relationship styles of two people who didn't learn healthy oxytocin responses from their families.

Art is a charming and successful guy who always has a woman in his life. At forty, he feels himself slipping into perpetual bachelorhood, even though he wants to settle down. "I just haven't found the right person," he says.

His last relationship, with Jennifer, was typical. "It seemed as if we had a great connection. She's smart and has the same quirky sense of humor I do," he says. Things seemed to be moving along nicely, and their first vacation together, four days in Cabo, was a blast.

But after that trip, things changed in some hard-to-define way. "I dunno," Art muses. "The spark died, and when it did, there didn't seem to be anything left." Art dropped Jennifer and freshened up his online dating profile.

Art's a healthy and attractive guy who has no trouble performing well in social and sexual situations. But "performance" is the right word. Art's parents were worried about spoiling him, so his mother let him cry and cry. From the beginning, he slept in his own bedroom; his wailing brought no comfort. Soon, he learned to cope by avoiding his feelings of loneliness and fear. His baby mind saw the world as a chilly place where no one offered help or support. As an adult, his emotional set point remains low.

Art's charm is a survival tactic. It enables him to get the resources he needs: jobs, acquaintances, bed partners. But his relationships are low in oxytocin. His emotional set point tends to keep people at a distance. He'll constantly monitor his emotional distance from friends, lovers, and family. He'll feel the beginnings of the oxytocin response as a dangerous loss of control. If he dates someone more secure, and she tries to draw him into intimacy, his emotional thermostat will shut down the relationship. "Too warm," it will tell him. "Move away."

Andrea is definitely a high-maintenance friend. Her girlfriends are used to getting her late-night calls, and they're willing to spend hours discussing every nuance of Andrea's romances—because they know they'll be making those same relationship calls to her. But men feel pressured by her anxiety and neediness.

"Men are so emotionally unavailable," Andrea complains. "All I want is one good man who'll be there for me—always." Although she approaches every new relationship with open arms, Andrea feels that the more she tries to be close, the more her partners pull away. The early stages of Andrea's love relationships are perfect. Her boyfriend's thrilled by her eagerness and delight in him. Then, things begin to subtly change. Her delight turns into criticism; little misunderstandings blow up into huge fights. The make-up sex is better than ever—until resentment begins to cool it. Sooner or later, there's the "Relationship Talk," and it always ends the same way. Andrea presses for commitment, and he runs.

Andrea's mother ran hot and cold. Sometimes, she'd be entranced by her baby, gazing delightedly into her eyes and stroking her silky hair as she drank from her bottle. It made Andrea ecstatic, shooting oxytocin and dopamine through her system. But Andrea's mother was a moody woman. After the initial excitement, she felt let down and trapped. She was left alone to take care of the dirty diapers, the rashes and sniffles, the endless bottles.

There were times, when Andrea was clean and quiet, when her mother doted on her perfect baby, and Andrea warmed in her love. But the love came and went. Andrea tried every baby trick she could to entice her mother, but she could never be sure of getting a response.

Andrea's emotional thermostat reflects that dynamic. She craves feeling the oxytocin response, but it comes with a load of anxiety. Close is never close enough. She's so hungry for attention and affirmation that even the most emotionally available people are unable to provide attention and reassurance she constantly craves.

Sylvie's friends say she can't commit. She had a steady boyfriend in high school, but when she got to college, she went a little man-crazy. She dated one guy after another, often dropping them after a couple of dates. Even now, her so-called relationships seldom last more than a couple of months. Men complain that she's a tease. She makes them jump through hoops just for a few kisses; getting her into bed's harder than writing a master's thesis.

Then Sylvie meets Marc. She's just as physically standoffish with him at first, but as that critical two-month period passes, they start spending even more time together. After six months, they make love, and it seals the relationship. When Marc graduates, he takes a job near the university, and they move in together. Now, they're planning their wedding.

Sylvie's mom and dad both came from large, extended families. When Sylvie was born, her grandmother moved in with the family. The house was crowded, but it was filled with life and love. The women passed Sylvie back and forth as they did chores and ran errands. When Sylvie's mother went back to work after family leave was over, it wasn't a hard transition for the baby, because Grandma was still there. Even her two older brothers helped out, playing with Sylvie on the floor while dinner was cooking.

Sylvie learned from the beginning that people were a source of emotional pleasure and comfort. Her oxytocin response grew strong, and that connected feeling was associated with no fear or pain. When she started dating, Sylvie could unconsciously compare her earliest experiences of intimacy with new relationships, and she automatically rejected any connection that didn't offer the same pleasure and security. When she met Marc, who could connect as deeply and securely as she could, she was drawn to him immediately. They took time to build trust in each other, and then bonded strongly.

Just Like Dear Old Dad

When you understand how the primary caregiver shapes the way your brain develops, it's not surprising that, when the dazzle of infatuation dissipates, the incredible babe you're romancing begins to remind you of Mom or Dad. It looks as if Mom and Dad—especially Mom— provide the basis for a working model of attachment that we begin with when we try to connect with someone new (Brumbaugh and Fraley 2007). But this model isn't carved in stone. Thanks to neural plasticity, the growth of new neurons, and the forging of new connections between them that remains throughout our lives, our brains continue to change in response to experience. And that gives us the opportunity to move into healthier kinds of attachment.

Chris Fraley and Claudia Brumbaugh of the University of Illinois have been tracking attachment styles for several years, via studies and Internet surveys. They've found that as we meet and get to know more and more people, we edit that original model of a relationship until it's more of an average of all our experiences of others. We may also develop some more specific models besides a parental figure, such as a friend or lover. Ideally, we continue to edit all these models based on our ongoing experiences in the world.

Do only babies born naturally and raised by stay-at-home moms have a chance at vigorous oxytocin responses, secure attachments, and connected lives? Of course not. In the past few years, neuroscientists have discovered that *neuroplasticity*—the ability of the brain to grow new neurons and make connections among them—continues throughout life. *We humans, with our wonderfully flexible brains, can learn to have a healthy oxytocin response at any stage of life. The cycle of failed attachment can be broken.*

Whether we remain stuck, using the unhealthy neural scripts we learned as babies, depends partly on luck. A mentor outside the family—whether a teacher, cleric, or friend—can enable a kid to expe-rience trust and intimacy that's not dangerous. This can also be the result of conscious effort. As we'll see in the next chapter, new circuits can grow, and we can learn the oxytocin response at any age.

The Attachment Dance
for Mothers and Caregivers

As babies, we learn some of the most crucial human skills from our mothers or other nurturers—including the ability to love and feel loved, to take stress in stride, and to face the world with joy. There's an emotional *pas de deux* between mother and baby that helps the baby's brain organize itself for love and commu-nication with others. Most mothers do it naturally and uncon-sciously. Paying attention to this interaction and setting aside regular time for it will strengthen the bond between you and your baby, heighten your own oxytocin response, and help the baby experience it.

To review, here's how the dance goes: As mother and baby look intensely into each other's eyes, their feelings of love and bonding increase as oxytocin, the hormone of love and trust, floods their bodies. The feelings swell to a crescendo, and then the baby typically will avert her gaze for a moment to process this intense emotion. Soon, the baby looks back again and begins another phase of engagement and deep feeling. This sweet interaction produces endorphins in the baby's brain that let him associate social interaction with pleasure—a crucial con-nection for forming adult relationships.

The Attachment Dance is not only for the primary caregiver and a baby. Any adult who's close to a child of any age, and especially another parent, should practice this sweet, nonverbal interaction to help the baby extend her circle of affection.

1. Set aside at least twenty minutes when you won't be disturbed. Turn off your phone, the television, the CD player, or anything distracting.

2. Sit comfortably with your baby in your arms. How do you feel? Some people may be anxious about not having entertainment, or worried about being

bored. That's okay. Allow yourself to experience those emotions.

3. Whether you feel anxious and bored or calm and happy, sit and watch your baby's face. Where do her eyes go? Focus on her facial expressions, her gestures, and any sounds she makes. Try to let go of naming these expressions or wondering what she's feeling, and just watch them.

4. Let her take the lead. Don't try to attract her attention. Wait until she looks at you. When she does, look back at her calmly. Check in with your body. Do you feel restless or relaxed? Interested or nervous?

5. Now, smile and talk to the baby. Stroke her, tickle her, and do all the things she likes. Watch what pleases her at this moment, and do more of it. Move with her into a state of *arousal*, that is, heightened awareness and intensity of feeling. Always try to match and amplify the baby's state.

6. At some point, your baby will naturally look away. Don't try to bring her attention back to you. Instead, examine your own state. Do you feel energized and more relaxed, or do you feel some tension now that the baby isn't engaged with you? Notice and accept these feelings while reminding yourself that this is part of a normal cycle of engagement and detachment that every person cycles through.

7. Be ready for when your baby once again looks into your face so that you can welcome the interaction warmly and again move with her into connection.

8. Move through the cycle of connection and detachment several times. End the session gently. If you can, keep the baby with you as you do other tasks. If you can't do that, be sure to end the Attachment Dance when the baby is in a calm state, not during a period of heightened arousal.

The Attachment Dance teaches your baby how to communicate emotional states, and also that it's natural to move from one state to another. Remind yourself—and others—that cuddle time isn't an indulgence; it's a necessity. Feel free to immerse yourself in baby bliss often. It's good for both of you.

The Attachment Dance *is based on the work of Allan Schore (2007) and others.*

Chapter 3

always the lonely

mothering is the first thing to shape the oxytocin response. So, as we grow, the whole world becomes a mirror of "Mother." When I reached out to be held, did she enfold me? Then I'll reach out to hold others. Was I warmed? Was I fed? Then I know the world will give me what I need, and I'll ask for what I want. Or, did she leave me alone to cry? Did she change my diapers roughly, with disgust? I'll remember the message clearly: I'm not worthy of love.

As we apply the oxytocin response we learned at Mother's breast to the people we meet, we repeat that first relationship over and over. The girl whose mothering came with a dose of rage will freak when that oxytocin feeling begins to trickle through her veins. She'll date boys who like to keep their distance, or angry ones. The boy who wasn't stroked and cuddled will define relationships in terms of competition or sex. Our oxytocin response may be so weak or thwarted that we never really connect at all. We may live in deep emotional isolation that colors everything we experience. If we marry, we're likely to marry someone who'll help recreate the kind of love we're used to. Together, we'll raise another generation of people who don't know how to love.

We don't need to stay stuck in these bleak emotional scripts, but unfortunately, we don't always get the tools to rewrite them. Any warm, trusting relationship can help the brain build up the oxytocin response, while psychotherapy—when it's a true *relationship*—can provide the practice it takes to develop new neural scripts. The barriers to change include those feelings of helplessness and hopelessness carried over from the time when we really *were* helpless as babies, and a competitive, increasingly hostile society in which people fear strangers and never get to know their neighbors. The incentive to change those neurochemical scripts is the opportunity to experience the deep connection we crave.

When Love Goes Wrong

It's so important to take action—to work to build a strong and healthy oxytocin response—because a lack of trust and love in our lives does much more than make us sad. Because of oxytocin's dual role in producing positive emotions and as one of the regulators of the parasympathetic nervous system, its lack can damage physical health and shorten life.

Ice-Colored Glasses

John Cacioppo may be the world's top expert on loneliness and the harm it does to health. The University of Chicago psychologist has spent his career uncovering the connection between emotion and physiology. He's discovered that, while we all experience bouts of loneliness and periods when circumstances take us out of our circles of support, loneliness can become an emotional and physical habit.

If you check in with people randomly throughout the day, asking them how things are going, the lonely and the non-lonely will have the same sorts of hassles or uplifts, with the same frequency. But the lonely ones will say that the hassles are more severe, and the uplifts less intense. They seem to have a cold blue filter over their emotions.

When Cacioppo and his colleague, Louise Hawkley, took a look at the social lives of 2,600 students, they found that the ones who scored highest for loneliness were also negative, anxious, and angry (2005).

They were more likely to see the world as punitive and to expect things to go badly. They saw adversity as a threat, not a challenge, and they reacted by running away. The least lonely scholars, compared with the loneliest, seemed to look at the world through rosier-colored glasses. These young people were more optimistic and outgoing. When things went wrong, they instinctively reached out to others for help and support. This difference seems to be rooted in the way their brains work.

When Cacioppo scanned people's brains as they looked at photos of happy couples that were unknown to them, he saw a big difference in which areas lit up. In the brains of non-lonely people, blood rushed to a large section of the *ventral tegmental area*, a part of the brain's reward system. Seeing two people smiling at each other made them feel good (Cacioppo et al., forthcoming). But lonely people didn't have this feel-good response. Lonely people may know intellectually that being with others is a good thing, but they don't *feel* it deep inside. The difference in quality of feeling, Cacioppo says, is like the difference in the way we respond to ice cream and twenty-four-hour banking. We know that being able to use an ATM is a great convenience, but it doesn't have the same zing as a cup of mocha gelato. "Both are equally good," he says, "but with the ice cream, I have an emotional response as well as an evaluative one" (Cacioppo 2007).

Cacioppo's team doesn't track it, but part of this emotional response is the release of oxytocin—the soothing, healing, regenerative hormone. Another part is dopamine—the rewarding, energizing, feel-good neurotransmitter. In other words, lonely people may consistently miss out on one of nature's best tonics for the body and nervous system. Without the balance of oxytocin, they're more prone to stress and to the negative effects of too much cortisol, the hormone of fight or flight.

Stressed Out

These icy filters don't color only our thoughts. Loneliness can take a physical toll as well. Researchers have already found strong evidence that lonely people can spiral into a vicious circle of disconnection and illness. Cortisol, the chemical that keeps us alert and helps us cope with stress, seems to be the culprit. Among the elderly people whom

Cacioppo and Hawkley studied, there's a clear link between loneliness and high cortisol (Cacioppo et al. 2000).

Cortisol is the yang to oxytocin's yin. The body needs a little boost to get it going after sleep, so the brain typically sends out a jolt of cortisol to wake us up. This *cortisol awakening response*, or CAR, is part of a daily ebb and flow that keeps us alert and able to cope with whatever comes our way. The cortisol level peaks in the first thirty to forty-five minutes after awakening, and then drops over the course of the day, reaching its lowest point around midnight.

The height of those peaks and the depth of those valleys are a part of each person's chemical signature. Stressed-out folks often show a higher CAR; in fact, they can have elevated cortisol levels all day long. While this chemical plays a vital role in regulating our physiologies, chronically high cortisol levels can lead to a host of physical ills. When your cortisol level is high, your body is stuck in fight-or-flight mode, the state that emphasizes near-term survival. For example, cortisol reduces the activity of *insulin*, the hormone that allows cells to absorb glucose from the blood. This is great when you need a sudden burst of energy, but when it's prolonged, you can develop insulin resistance, the first stage of type 2 diabetes. Cortisol also constricts the veins and arteries, raising blood pressure, reducing the ability to heal injuries of the blood vessels, and increasing the likelihood of the blood clots that can lead to stroke. Finally, it limits the body's general healing response (Walker 2007).

A 2006 study Cacioppo and Hawkley did with Emma Adam of Northwestern University and Brigitte Kudielka of the University of Trier showed how we can spiral down into loneliness and ill health: one day's emotional experiences set the next day's endocrine tone (Adam et al. 2006). They sent 156 older adults home with bags full of plastic tubes and multipage questionnaires. The participants spit into the tubes three times a day, and they also answered dozens of questions that exhaustively catalogued their routines, from whether they ate junk food to whether they got support from the person closest to them, from a pet, or from God.

It turned out that one bad day can lead to another stressed-out day. People who reported feeling overwhelmed, sad, threatened, or lonely had higher cortisol levels when they woke up the following day. "If yesterday was so crummy," their bodies seemed to say, "I'd better prepare for a worse day today." The resulting jangle of extra cortisol could make them jumpier and more likely to *have* angry interactions, and less likely to notice or respond to positive overtures from others. This constant state of fight or flight wears down the body. In the short term, the extra jolt of cortisol after a bad day may get you over the hump. In the long run, though, it turns into a killer, because it keeps us from reaching out to get the soothing we need.

high pressure

In Cacioppo's lab at the University of Chicago Center for Cognitive and Social Neuroscience, researchers chart the merest twitch of a muscle, a few extra drops of blood to a section of the brain, and the delay of a heartbeat to understand what they call *social endocrinology*: how being with people—or being cut off from them—changes the chemical brew that infuses the brain.

The monitoring setup looks like a music recording studio: racks of hardware with sliders and knobs, and a row of video monitors. But this rig is recording the music of human emotion, as expressed in the peaks and pulses of electrical activity. The heart of the lab is an enclosed room behind a forbiddingly solid door. Its four-inch thickness blocks out sound, while copper strips lining the jamb and the door's edge snag stray electrical impulses that could interfere with the delicate sensors inside. This monitoring room is as pleasantly nondescript as a dentist's waiting room, except for the huge flat-panel TV screen. It has a comfy upholstered wing chair, a coffee table with a few magazines, and a side chair. The only indication of its function is a snake of cables coming through the wall behind the armchair.

Inside this room, Jia Cheng winds sticky metallic tape around my neck several times, and then again around my waist. She's about to hook me up to a battery of sensors that will track how I respond to the embarrassment of making mistakes in front of a stranger. If I were a study participant, by this time I would've completed a questionnaire that let the research team measure my level of loneliness: how connected I felt to others and how much support I believed I had to face problems large and small. As their database of such questionnaires grows, they can chart how stressed the lonely and the connected become.

Cheng, one of the lab's project managers, attaches the end of each magnetic strip stuck to my body to a sensor, straps a blood-pressure cuff to my left arm, and straps another monitor to my wrist to follow my pulse. Then the fun begins. Zach Johnson, another project manager, enters the room, sits on the chair at my left side, and gives me a no-nonsense look. He tells me I'll perform a mental subtraction test, and he'll judge my performance. I've read about this test, designed to turn up the heat, so I'm not too alarmed about my performance—but still, I'm not looking forward to the math.

The first couple of sets seem relatively easy, but by the fourth round, my brain is seriously tired. I have trouble remembering the number I'm supposed to subtract, and sometimes my mind just stalls: "What *is* 738 minus 7?" All the time, the sensing equipment monitors changes in my physical state. I breathe a sigh of relief when the last round comes, and 3 is the number I need to subtract. (Evidently, this puts me at barely average in my math ability; testers adjust the difficulty as the test progresses to make sure it's stressful enough. Some people need to be asked to serially subtract 17 to become stressed.)

My test isn't exactly fair. I know what the game is, so I don't have the same kind of performance anxiety someone else might experience. But the point of the study isn't to determine any individual's reaction. Instead, Cacioppo and Hawkley are looking for patterns. Do people who are lonelier, for example, become stressed sooner? Do they exhibit more stress when trying to subtract 8 from 1,297 than people who say they have many people they can turn to? They've found that lonely people are more likely to have high blood pressure as they age (Hawkley et al. 2006), and they're more at risk for depression (Cacioppo et al. 2006). In fact, loneliness can accelerate the aging process itself (Hawkley and Cacioppo 2007).

Nonetheless, Cacioppo and Hawkley don't see loneliness as a negative state. They see it as part of our brain's signaling system. Just as hunger signals us to go to the fridge, loneliness tells us it's time to connect with someone else.

The Anti-Cortisol

Across town from Cacioppo's operation, in Sue Carter's lab at the University of Illinois, they've demonstrated how oxytocin acts as an anti-cortisol. In an unpublished 2007 study led by Angela Grippo (Carter 2007b), researchers isolated female prairie voles for four weeks. Isolation is intensely distressing to these little beasts, which normally live huddled together in family groups. After two weeks in "solitary," they gave some of the lonely voles a daily dose of oxytocin. These critters showed much better regulation of their heart rates in general, and their hearts didn't pound as hard when they were stressed by the introduction of a strange vole.

But it's not as simple as "more oxytocin equals less stress." Another 2007 study by Carter's crew (Grippo, Cushing, and Carter 2007) illustrates the contradictory nature of oxytocin levels. When researchers isolated prairie voles for several weeks, they expected oxytocin levels to go down. Instead, the voles' oxytocin levels went up. The brain seems to pump out oxytocin in times of stress, and perhaps, Carter thinks, this flush acts as a signal to look for social support (2007b).

In fact, you could think of loneliness as a craving for oxytocin. Just as a healthy body seeks food to satisfy hunger, it seeks out other people to satisfy its hunger for physical and emotional connection. People with healthy oxytocin responses are open and eager for connection. The bonds they form help them cope with stress so that a bad day doesn't seem as bad. At the same time, they invite more connection, because they're oblivious to other people's crankiness, and able to smooth ruffled feathers and attract more positive interactions with their smiles.

The Cycle of Failed Attachment

The problem is, this loneliness signal is as subject to going haywire as hunger is. Anorexics don't follow their bodies' urges to eat, and some of us learned that reaching out leads to rejection or pain. When you were a toddler, you quickly realized that "hot" meant a painful burn. You naturally snatched your hand away when Daddy said it, and soon you began to understand that you should approach anything warm with a little vigilance. Those of us with "hot" parents—snappish mothers, yelling fathers—learn to approach others with the same caution.

When you grow up in a family where getting close means being hurt, that oxytocin feeling itself can become a warning signal. A kind word or a friendly touch may trigger the oxytocin response, but instead of feeling calm and happy, our brains say, "Uh oh. It's time to get out of here."

So, what kind of people *will* feel safe to you? The ones who don't evoke the oxytocin response. Thus, in your attempts to feel safe, you end up disconnected.

The lonely can fall into a state of perpetual distrust and pessimism that colors their world and reinforces their loneliness. They find betrayal where others see negligence. They expect the worst from strangers and belittle the support they do receive from friends and lovers.

Certainly, these attitudes are self-reinforcing, pushing away the emotionally open people who might befriend the lonely. Lonely people tend to see the people around them in a bad light—and their acquaintances pick up on it and dislike them in return (Cacioppo et al. 2000). The walking wounded seem to travel through life on the same path as everyone else, but every day, they drink from a deep well of loneliness. Some may marry and raise families; others may drift through the tides of ever-changing relationships, unable to "find the right person." They're lonely in a crowded room. Even when they do find love and intimacy, the calming effect of oxytocin may not be able to overcome the high levels of stress hormones that keep their nervous systems twanging.

A Rising Tide of Pain

This state of isolation may become our national character. We seem to be brewing a national tragedy, raising generations that are each more damaged and less able to love than the previous.

In 2001, a group of experts on child development and health surveyed the state of America's children. The results were frightening: one of every four adolescents in the United States is at serious risk of not achieving productive adulthood (Kline and the Commission on Children at Risk 2003). The report emphasized the role of oxytocin in bonding, acknowledging how nurturing shapes the brain. And it identified an alarming trend. In a nation of great wealth and immense disparity in access to education and resources, we're breeding kids who can't connect. Their neurochemistries are out of whack, juiced up with fight-or-flight chemicals but sadly deficient in the ability to respond to oxytocin.

The study, by the Commission on Children at Risk, found rising rates of depression; anxiety; attention deficit and conduct disorders; suicide; and other serious mental, emotional, and behavioral problems among children and adolescents. Since the 1950s, it found, death rates from disease or injury have fallen by about 50 percent among youth, while homicide rates have risen by more than 130 percent. Suicide rates have risen by nearly 140 percent; suicide is now the third leading cause of death among young people in the United States.

The statistics are dire. According to the commission—a panel of thirty-three doctors, neuroscientists, researchers, and youth services professionals—21 percent of children aged nine to seventeen had a diagnosable mental or addictive disorder; 20 percent of students reported having seriously considered suicide in the past year. The report concluded that this generation of youth is much more likely to be depressed and anxious than its parents' generation was.

The commission laid the blame on two things: a lack of enough close connections to other people, and a societal disconnect from morals and spiritual meaning. It pointed out that, as our children's emotional health has worsened, social institutions that could provide connection to the community and to shared values, such as churches and schools, have gotten weaker.

Unlovable?

Sometimes the damage to children from a lack of love and care is even more severe. In cases where one suffers true neglect or abuse, the oxytocin response may be so underdeveloped that the child's system gets locked in the fight-or-flight response. When this happens, the child may engage in the kind of destructive and violent behavior that pushes her parents over the edge. There's now a name for this: *reactive attachment disorder*, or *RAD*, a controversial psychiatric label that was added to the *Diagnostic and Statistical Manual of Mental Disorders* (*DSM*) in

2000. The *DSM* is the psychiatric "bible," allowing professionals to classify mental disorders in a standardized way.

The basic criterion for a diagnosis of RAD is, "markedly disturbed and developmentally inappropriate social relatedness in most contexts" (American Psychiatric Association 2000, 127). These kids may be extremely withdrawn, painfully anxious, or ambivalent about receiving attention and love. They may also be indiscriminate in their affection, happy to climb into strangers' laps and seemingly ready to go home with anyone.

Fundamentally, RAD kids are unable to bond with their parents. They're like flower seeds planted in concrete. They're unable to absorb the love they're offered—and they're furious about this. There's another criterion for diagnosing RAD: the child didn't get the care he needed at a critical time—from birth through the first three months of life. According to the *DSM*, RAD is caused by the persistent disregard of the child's basic emotional needs for comfort, stimulation, and affection; disregard for his physical needs; or repeated changes in caregivers that never gave him time to bond with anyone.

The *DSM* puts the blame for this disorder squarely on the caretakers who failed the child. Mothers who, themselves, were traumatized by abuse, or who suffer from drug addiction, alcoholism, or extreme poverty, can be incapable of providing the safety and care a baby needs. Their children may fall into "the system," shuffling through a succession of hospitals, state facilities, and foster homes, where they never get a chance to connect with anyone.

Learning to Connect

Most of us have been lucky enough to avoid the trauma of abuse or neglect. And yet, this description of RAD may resonate a bit. Maybe you're not painfully withdrawn, but your first impulse is to shy away from intimacy. You may feel so anxious about your relationships that you can't enjoy them, or maybe you find it hard to believe that anyone would love you. Or perhaps you've been a bit indiscriminate in your love life, going home with exciting princes who turn out to be frogs. These milder relationship problems could be symptoms of a weakened attachment system: a weak oxytocin response as the result of a less-than-optimal emotional environment when you were a child.

Psychotherapy of many kinds can actually retrain the brain and build the oxytocin response. Next, we'll look at examples of therapeutic interventions that go beyond the cognitive level to change our neuro-chemical reactions.

Breaking the Cycle

Some lucky mothers who weren't mothered well themselves find their way into programs that help break the cycle of failed attachment. Because we learn what we can expect from our parents emotionally long before we have the ability to form memories or analyze our experiences, it's really hard for us to understand how mothering can hurt. The Circle of Security (COS) project, based at the Marycliff Institute in Spokane, Washington, aims to let a mother uncover the insecurity and pain she felt when she was a child (Hoffman et al. 2006). Once she sees how her own old hurts prevent her from giving her child what he needs, she can begin to help him feel secure and loved. In effect, COS teaches these mothers emotional regulation, enabling them to not only cool down their babies' limbic systems but also keep from responding to the babies' distress by becoming anxious or angry themselves (Powell 2006).

The COS founders, Kent Hoffman, Robert Marvin, Glen Cooper, and Bert Powell, created an easy-to-understand model of the different attachment styles, along with some intuitive ways to describe what's unconsciously going on between mother and child. Before a COS group begins, each mother and child pair is videotaped in Mary Ainsworth's "Strange Situation," the scenario that helps uncover their attachment styles. Mothers also participate in a videotaped interview. Mothers meet in groups of six, weekly for twenty weeks. In the sessions, they watch videotapes of mother-child interactions, edited by COS therapists to illustrate not only the central problem in the relationship but also times when the mother is successful in giving her child what he needs.

The COS team came up with a visceral metaphor to explain how a mom's emotional baggage can interfere with her ability to see her child as he really is. They show the women a video clip of a beautiful coastal rainforest set to two kinds of music. First, serene, soothing music plays, and the women discuss the pleasant feelings it evokes. Next, the ominous music from *Jaws* plays, and as the mothers talk about the anxious feelings the same placid scene now evokes, they understand how their own emotional tone colors the way they see their kids.

"Shark music" becomes a useful metaphor for moments when a mother is reacting to her own sensitivities instead of her child's needs. As they watch the tapes of themselves and the other mother-child pairs in the group, each woman begins to identify when a kid is "miscuing," that is, trying to disguise the need to be mothered so as not to trigger Mommy's pain. Each mother learns to separate her child's longing from her own, and to give the love she never got.

In response, her baby learns to turn to her for love and comfort. He learns, at the somatic level, that if he can be close to someone, his brain will release soothing, healing oxytocin, and he'll feel better. As he grows older, he'll be able to turn to other people for love and support.

COS therapists score each child's attachment style during the Strange Situation assessment and again after the twenty-week COS program is completed. It looks as if this program can help even the most desperately disconnected kids create a secure attachment style by the end of the program. In one study of sixty-five toddlers, the majority shifted to secure attachment (Hoffman et al. 2006).

While most COS projects involve what are known as "at-risk" women—homeless mothers, mothers in prison, and mothers with a history of violence—there's a project in Perth, Australia, working in a hospital perinatal unit to foster secure attachments from the very beginning. Powell and his colleagues in Washington have worked with babies and kids up to five years old. Powell thinks the sweet spot for intervention is when the baby is two or three months old, so that the mother has had time to get to know the child but the negative behavior patterns haven't become entrenched (2006). But even the most vulnerable of mothers seems to be able to make the subtle changes that can turn a tormented child into one who knows she's loved.

Megan runs her fingers along the collection of dolls and figurines that lines the wall of Sally Clark's office. The five-year-old's parents are separated and divorcing. For eight months when she was two, Megan was a client of Clark, a therapist in Albany,

California, who specializes in working with children and adults to heal prenatal, birth, and attachment trauma; now Megan's back with her mom to help her handle this major shake-up. (Her name and some details have been changed to protect her privacy.)

Megan is a charmer who seems to know she can rely on her mother, casually climbing into her lap or throwing a leg over her as she talks to Clark about her dress. Soon, she goes to the sand tray, a shallow, three-foot-square box, and begins to pick out objects from the hundreds arrayed on five shallow shelves. She places a tiny ceramic aquarium bridge in the center of the sand. "It's land under the bridge, not water," she says. She arranges two pavilions toward the center, and places a paper tepee in the right-front corner. Into each house goes a little dog. Soon, the tray is full of objects. A Marilyn Monroe figure, leaning over to give a sexy kiss, faces an androgynous doll with boots and a sword. In the back-left corner, two black mummy cases represent the mother and grandmother, who died. Behind them, a lighthouse pokes up.

Megan points to a tiny toy. "This dog is lost," she says. "He needs his mommy."

"Can you find someone to take care of him?" asks Clark, providing some direction for the first time.

Megan picks out the figure of a woman holding a swaddled baby, and places it near the dog. It keeps falling over, so Clark moves another piece to hold it up.

Megan doesn't want to tell a story about the scene she's created. "I'm not good at stories," she says. But she spends a few minutes drawing a picture of a sun, a woman's face with huge grinning teeth, and a little dog in one corner. Finally, she and her mom snuggle in a cushioned, curtained alcove.

There's plenty to interpret in Megan's *mise-en-scène*. The mummy caskets could represent the death of the marriage; the bridge might stand for this family transition; the tepee seems to represent a safe home or perhaps the womb itself. In addition to the problem at hand, her parents' impending divorce may also trigger memories of earlier attachment trauma hidden in Megan's right hemisphere. Clark will discuss all this with Megan's mother, and provide some suggestions about how to support the girl through this difficult period.

But the interpretation is secondary, Clark says. What will help Megan cope isn't Clark's insights but the opportunity Megan had to communicate in a safe environment. Explains Clark, "It's not the interpretation. It's that she expressed herself and was heard" (Clark 2007).

Clark's work illustrates the way healing takes place below the conscious level. Babies and children this age don't have the cognitive and verbal skills to understand and talk about the fright and distress of their earliest experiences, which are lodged in the emotional memory of the right hemisphere. But they can express it, and play is a direct channel to that hemisphere. Clark and Megan are communicating limbic system to limbic system, according to Allan Schore, a UCLA professor of psychology and author of *Affect Regulation and the Repair of the Self* (2003). It's that state of limbic resonance, where they're attuned, on the same wavelength. When this happens, Clark's mature nervous system can take charge and let Megan's nervous system experience the journey from arousal to fear to calm again.

As Schore explains it, the pairing of traumatic feelings with the context of safety and support gives Clark's patients not just a reenactment but an actual new experience, the experience of feeling frightened or angry, and being comforted and loved (Schore 2007).

Why Therapy Works

Talking about feelings is like trying to write poetry with a banana; the prefrontal cortex is the wrong tool for the job. The reason just talking over attachment problems doesn't make them go away is that these patterns and reactions were learned before conscious memory developed. Language and logical thought processes are handled by the prefrontal cortex in the left hemisphere, the last part of the brain to come online. Feelings and autonomic responses to our experiences, on the other hand, are the province of the right hemisphere, the site of the first brain functions to develop.

That's not to say that traditional talk therapy can't work. But when it does work, it works at the unconscious level. Healing happens because of the *relationship*, not because of what you say to your therapist. Freud called this special relationship "the therapeutic alliance," and he dubbed the process whereby a patient recreates early emotional experiences in this relationship "transference." Schore sees the right hemisphere as the neural structure that's representative of Freud's "unconscious." Today, transference is an accepted part of most kinds of therapies—and the most crucial element of its effectiveness, Schore says (Schore 2007).

The therapist and the patient form an attachment that's based in that unconscious, not-thinking-but-feeling right hemisphere. The therapist gives the patient something she never had before, someone who not only listens and understands but who can also communicate body to body, at the level of the autonomic nervous system.

As they work together, the patient's emotional responses will come, not from thoughts or insights but from the implicit emotional system of the right hemisphere. At first, this new relationship will likely take the same dysfunctional form that the patient is prone to use. As the patient responds to the therapist's words, actions, and emotions, her amygdala will send her body into the same states it fell into as a baby.

The therapist's task is to keep the patient from falling into a state of panic and emergency by offering the mirroring, comfort, and security that weren't available to her as a baby. To make this work, the therapist has to *participate*. He must allow himself to actually experience the patient's emotions in his own body, and then take on the task of not only regulating his own emotions but also the client's. At these times, the therapist who can meet the patient body to body, right hemisphere to right hemisphere, actually joins her in her emotional state as it's expressed in their physiologies. Then, if they're in tune, the patient's body can follow the therapist's out of the high-cortisol, high-stress state and let the parasympathetic nervous system gradually take over, releasing oxytocin. This attunement between the two gives the client's brain a new model for healthy self-regulation, a pattern it eventually makes its own.

The relationship may be led by the therapist, but it's cocreated; the patient plays an equal part. And this cocreated emotional alliance actually leads to changes in the internal structure and chemical state of the patient's brain. In the privacy and safety of the therapist's office, the client can experience the combination of moderate arousal and nurturing that she missed or didn't get enough of. Eventually, this kind of psychotherapy can actually retrain the brain, making new connections and replacing the habit of fear or isolation with the ability to turn to others in order to share joy and soothe pain. The oxytocin response becomes a familiar friend.

No matter what form or technique of psychotherapy a practitioner uses, neuroscience has shown that creating a relationship with the patient that lets her practice new ways of reacting to fear or anger in ever-increasing doses actually repairs the damaged systems of the brain (Etkin et al. 2005). Researchers can watch how someone's brain functions as she moves through different emotional states, looking at photos of angry faces or videotapes of her baby laughing, and recalling sad times. They can compare her brain activity to the norm, and track how that changes over time. Such studies of people being treated for depression or obsessive-compulsive disorder have shown that therapy causes differences in blood flow to different parts of the brain, for example, increased activity of neurons in some areas and decreases in the activity of the amygdala, the brain's fear center. Of course, long before brain-imaging technology came around, we could tell if therapy was working. Those changes in the brain are reflected by changes in our behavior.

Puppy Love

You don't need to be in therapy to engage in relationships that help you tune your oxytocin response. You don't even need another human. Dogs are willing and effective partners: they're nonjudgmental, they follow your lead, and they'll never make fun of you behind your back. Many people believe their pets love them as much as they love their pets. There's evidence that this is true—at least in the case of dogs. Taking care of a dog or receiving its unqualified admiration can provoke the oxytocin response.

Johannes Odendaal was a South African veterinarian who was always fascinated by the role of companion animals in our society. He felt that there was something deeper in the relationship than the need for food and shelter on the animal's part. When he became a professor at Pretoria's Life Sciences Institute, he got an opportunity to test his theories. With his collaborator, R. A. Meintjes, he did the first—and what seems to be the only—experiment to measure *interspecific affiliation*, that is, the bond between a human and another species.

In 2003, Odendaal and Meintjes measured the blood levels of several chemicals, including endorphins, oxytocin, and dopamine—the chemicals of relaxation and pleasure—and cortisol, the stress hormone, in both people and dogs. They did the blood tests before and after the human-dog pairs played and cuddled together. They also compared the people's neurochemicals after they had petted their own dogs, after they had petted an unfamiliar dog, and after they had sat quietly and read a book.

In both humans and dogs, those chemicals of pleasure rose after five to twenty-four minutes of petting. The human subjects' oxytocin increased more when they interacted with their own dogs than with strange dogs. This result falls in line with the theory that interacting with intimates is one of the best oxytocin-boosters. In addition, the people's cortisol levels fell as they enjoyed their pets. The dogs' cortisol remained the same, possibly because they found this new environment interesting and fun.

An evolutionary biologist would argue that the funny tricks and cute wiggles that make our dogs seem so adorable developed over time to better a canine's chances of getting flung a scrap from a meal. The more a dog could appeal to his human companions, the better chance it had to be allowed into the shelter, to supplement its own foraging with a bit from the meager food store in the camp, and to avoid being eaten itself when times were desperate. This companionable dog was more likely to survive long enough to raise pups to adulthood, pups that would pass along its genetic tendencies to be adorable.

Fair enough—but some people take the view that dogs wear these cute actions as obliviously as the skunk wears his dazzling coat or the butterfly its gorgeous spots. Odendaal's study shows otherwise. Maybe it wasn't enough for those ancestral dogs to simply *act* as if they liked humankind; the ones with the best chance of survival and reproduction were those that could form a true emotional bond with their masters. A dog that felt the regenerative flow of oxytocin when it was stroked would stay closer to its master, come to him more often, and respond more to his touch. And as human stroked dog, he, too, felt the flow and was warmed and comforted.

When you define emotions as physiological states instead of psychological processes, and then identify a similar state in human and animal, it only makes sense to say that man and dog feel the same.

In any case, this study shows the physiological basis for the well-documented health benefits of pet ownership. Pet owners are less likely to develop heart disease, and if they do, they're more likely to survive a heart attack. They're better able to deal with the loss of a loved one, and have a better general sense of well-being (Friedmann 1991).

In fact, a dog may offer better emotional support than a person. In one study, researchers measured the blood pressure of female college students when they worked on complicated math problems in their own homes and in the lab (Allen et al. 1991). (An increase in blood pressure is a reliable measure of stress.) One group did the math with their dogs by their side; the other group worked in the presence of a girlfriend. Unsurprisingly, all the women solving math problems in the lab got a bit stressed. When they attempted to solve the problems at home, however, they got more stressed out with a friend peering over their shoulders than when only the researcher was present. Talk about peer pressure! The group that worked with their faithful, adoring dogs at their sides was the least stressed of all.

This study illustrates why a relationship with a dog can be a wonderful first step to opening up to other humans. Dogs don't judge us, and their demands are simple and easily met. Keeping that warm, furry body close and available for stroking; looking into those soulful brown eyes; feeling a warm tongue on your hand, neck, or chin recreates the experience of safe intimacy you may have missed as a baby. At the same time, taking care of a dog lets you practice nurturing yourself, which is another important part of the oxytocin response. Experiencing the oxytocin bond with a dog as you successfully meet its needs will give you a sense of what it should feel like to be close to another person—maybe for the first time in your life.

Cat owners seem to gain similar cardiovascular benefits to dog owners, so it's likely that any furry pet will do (Friedmann 1991). But fuzzy matters. Humans crave contact comfort with something warm and soft, and there's nothing like burying your fingers—and maybe your face—in soft fur.

Of course, having a pet brings its own set of stressors. Cats might poop on your bed, dogs demand walks, and even rabbits need their cages cleaned. Many of us feel maxed out with responsibilities already, so there's no way we can take on one more; blood pressure be damned.

Luckily, you can get your oxytocin fix without having a live-in animal companion. Many studies have proven the calming effects of other peoples' dogs (Friedmann 1991). And dogs are everywhere. A stroll in the park should provide plenty of opportunities for a pat and a wag; most cities have special dog-running areas where pets and people gather to socialize—and there's no law that says you need to be accompanied by your own.

For a more orderly interaction, volunteer at your local animal shelter. Animal advocates have recognized that pets in shelters quickly become depressed and anxious, which makes them seem less appealing to prospective owners. So shelters across the States have instituted programs that bring people in to comfort them. At the Berkeley-East Bay Humane Society, near where I live in California, volunteers need just a single two-hour orientation, and then they're invited to stop by at any time to spend as long or as little as they like visiting the dogs and cats. They talk to them, scratch their ears, and coax them out of corners with kibble. These volunteers give homeless animals the soothing benefits of touch. They may not realize it, but they're also invoking their own healing oxytocin response. Maybe someday, doctors will prescribe a session with a pet instead of a blood-pressure pill.

The Attachment Dance for Adults

You can practice the attachment dance from chapter 2 with another adult to strengthen your own oxytocin response. Choose someone you feel comfortable with—but you don't need to tell the other person about the exercise if you don't want to. You're simply intentionally doing something that we do unconsciously all the time.

1. Pick a quiet time and a situation where it's natural for you two to be face to face, such as sitting at a café or talking in your living room.

2. Begin to notice when you two look into each other's eyes, and when one of you looks away. Give yourself permission to look away whenever you feel like it.

3. Now, intentionally hold your friend's gaze for a few moments. Check in with your body. Is your breathing slow, or do you feel a constriction in your chest? Do your muscles feel tense or relaxed? Are you leaning back, sitting upright, or leaning forward?

4. When you feel like it, let your gaze move around again. You may look at your friend's mouth or her hands, or at something else in your environment.

5. Look back at your friend and notice when she returns your gaze. If it feels natural, say something positive about her or your relationship. If this doesn't feel comfortable, say it to yourself. You might think something as simple as, "I like you" or "You're a good person."

6. Notice how your body feels now. Is there any change? You may feel some muscle tension, or you may feel relaxation in some part of your body. Whatever you experience is okay.

7. Repeat the process for as long as it feels right.

The idea of this exercise is not necessarily to establish some deeper interpersonal connection with your friend—although that might happen, and if it does, it's very nice. The purpose is to practice staying in your comfort zone as you draw closer and then retreat a bit from connection. Every time you experience the cycle of engagement and disengagement, you learn that it can be safe to connect. The attachment dance lets grown-ups revisit or experience for the first time the interactions that teach the brain how to move into limbic resonance and enjoy the oxytocin response.

As you've seen, no one needs to live a life without the love and connection he or she needs. Understanding the cycle of failed attachment allows us to break it. Neuroplasticity, the ability of the brain to grow new neurons and make new connections among them, continues throughout life. The womb and the birth process are only the first of the many experiences that will shape the brain's ability to love, so change and healing can begin at any time. An anxious lover can blossom and become more secure in the warmth of a secure lover. He who dismisses intimacy as a trap for the weak can learn to accept its blessings. We can all learn to love.

In the last chapter of this book, we'll look at more ways to develop the oxytocin response in everyday life. But first, we'll look at how the oxytocin response plays a role in romance, committed love, and parenting. Think of these next chapters as your guidebook to forming fulfilling relationships.

How Lonely Are You?

It's hard to be objective about your feelings. When you're down, it feels as if you'll never smile again. When you feel alone, it seems as if you don't have a friend in the world. This test was developed by Daniel W. Russell, Ph.D., a professor at Iowa State University, to measure a person's level of loneliness. It will give you an idea of whether the feelings of disconnection you sometimes experience are part of normal life, or whether you need to work on building or reinvigorating your emotional network.

To take the test, read the statements describing how people sometimes feel. For each statement, indicate how often you feel the way described by writing a number in the space provided.

For example:

How often do you feel happy?

NEVER	RARELY	SOMETIMES	USUALLY
1	2	3	4

If you've felt happy sometimes but not usually, you would write the number 3. If you've never felt happy, you would write 1; if you usually feel happy, you would write 4 in the space next to that question.

1. How often do you feel unhappy doing so many things alone? ____

2. How often do you feel you have no one to talk to?
____

3. How often do you feel you cannot tolerate being so alone? ____

4. How often do you feel as if no one understands you? ____

5. How often do you find yourself waiting for people to call or write? ____

6. How often do you feel completely alone? ____

7. How often do you feel unable to reach out and communicate with those around you? ____

8. How often do you feel starved for company? ____

9. How often do you feel it is difficult for you to make friends? ____

10. How often do you feel shut out and excluded by others? ____

Scoring: Add up the numbers for your total score.

10–19: You feel connected and secure.

20–24: You're like most people who take this test.

25–29: You tend to feel more lonely than most people.

30–40: You experience a very high level of loneliness.

If you scored 25 or higher, try to make a conscious effort to connect with others. First, take a look at your daily life. Have you let work, school, or other responsibilities eat up all your time? Is there some situation that's taken you away from people you're close to, such as moving to a new city? Next, think of all the people you can count on for support, from family and loved ones to colleagues to casual acquaintances, who are good for a smile and a laugh. Do you simply need to make more of an effort to touch base with these folks, or is it time to put some work into building bridges to others? Do you need to strengthen your oxytocin response itself in order to enjoy connection?

Reprinted with permission from Daniel W. Russell, Ph.D., professor, Institute for Social and Behavioral Research, and Department of Human Development and Family Studies, Iowa State University. Originally published as UCLA loneliness scale (version 3): Reliability, validity, and factor structure, *Journal of Personality Assessment* 66 (1):20–40, 1996.

Throughout this book, and especially in the last chapter, you'll find ideas and exercises to improve your brain's ability to release oxytocin in times of safety and intimacy, as well as to create opportunities to enjoy oxytocin every day.

Chapter 4

romance: the first step to commitment

First comes love; then comes marriage. Then comes a baby in a baby carriage. This old hopscotch jingle is actually a scientific analysis of the three stages of human bonding: the spark of lust; intense, romantic attraction; and the sweet deepening of committed love. Although these stages of human bonding are connected, they use different brain systems, and they're ruled by different neurochemical cocktails (Fisher at al. 2002).

Unfortunately, popular culture has come to define romance, the fevered mix of lust and attraction, as "true love," relegating other kinds of attachment—including the deeply committed love of longtime partners—to pale imitations. But it may be a mistake to even include this madly romantic stage in our concept of love, because the chemistry that connects us in these phases is really different. There's one central neurochemical thread, however, that leads from sex to commitment: oxytocin, the neurochemical of bonding, is also a hormone that's essential to sex. Nature seems to have designed lust and attraction to allow people to overcome their fear of strangers enough to come together to procreate. As the excitement dissipates, the committed, oxytocin-based bond remains. This chapter will explain the chemistry of romance: how sexual interest leads to that focused state of excitement and attraction we call romance—and why it's quite different from what we might call true love or committed love.

Getting Together

Attraction, both sexual and emotional, is such a big part of life that we don't notice how surprising it is. While you may take weeks or months to make friends with someone or develop a trusting relationship with work colleagues, a single evening with a stranger can be enough to create visions of a life together. Sexual attraction—lust—is what gets us over that hump.

Lust: The Spark

The sex drive is one of the strongest forces in nature; quite simply, it evolved to drive every animal to procreate. In the complex human brain, with its bias toward social relationships, it manifests itself as lust. Lust can be indiscriminate or excruciatingly specific. It's associated with testosterone in both men and women, and it seems to travel a different path in the brain from that of courtship and committed love, although there is some overlap (Fisher, Aron, and Brown 2006). The sex drive is focused, quite simply, on intercourse with another individual.

Imagine how hard it would be to move into the home of someone you'd never met before and share his or her bed. And yet, sometimes, we'll gladly take off our clothes and copulate with people with whom we've had only minor social contact. The difference is in the stew of exciting neurochemicals that infuse the brain when its lust system becomes activated. In the first stage of love, lust—the drive for sex—serves to draw two people together, making them want to connect deeply on every level.

Lust doesn't need to be present for romantic feelings to develop. While it's perfectly possible to have sex with someone you don't feel romantic about, you can also be intensely passionate about someone you're not ready to have sex with. Adolescent crushes are an example of how we humans separate lust and romance, as were the courtly Middle Ages romances between knights and ladies. But lust can be the inflammatory factor that leads to courtship, the romantic pursuit of another.

Courtship: The Chase

While lust can well up in response to anything or nothing, romance homes in on one individual who becomes more desirable than any other—the one and only. Helen Fisher, a Rutgers anthropologist who studies romantic love using brain scans, says human romantic love is the equivalent to the process of mate selection that takes place throughout the animal kingdom (Fisher 1998). While lust propels us toward a sexual connection, romance propels us to emotional—and probably sexual—connection with a particular individual.

Most animals engage in courtship, a series of behaviors that demonstrates an individual's worthiness as a genetic partner, as well as its ability to successfully provide for and defend the precious offspring. Fisher says that the human equivalent, which we designate as romance, involves the same elements: a sense of high energy and excitement, attention focused on the object of desire, possessiveness and a desire to be in close contact, and the motivation to do whatever it takes to win his or her love (2004).

What differentiates romantic love from lust, according to Fisher (2004), is that in the former, the lover's craving for emotional union seems more important and more valuable than the desire for sexual union.

fear of the unknown

Aside from the innate and social differences between men and women, the process of falling in love requires us to become extremely vulnerable to a stranger. When you think about it, it *is* rather amazing that we're so willing to consider forming a lifelong bond with someone we barely know. While testosterone-fueled desire impels us over the brink, oxytocin also helps ease the transition between stranger and lover—but not exactly as you might expect.

In a 2006 study, Donatella Marazziti and her team at the University of Pisa looked at the relationship between levels of oxytocin in the blood and anxiety in romantic relationships—and what they found was counterintuitive. You'd expect people in secure, happy relationships to be awash in oxytocin, while people embroiled in worries about their relationships suffer from its lack. But, it was just the opposite.

First, they gave the forty-five subjects in the study a questionnaire known as "Experiences in Close Relationships." This test assesses the style of attachment a person typically forms in relationships. It expands the three attachment styles—secure, avoidant, and anxious—into four: preoccupied, dismissing, fearful or avoidant, and secure.

Preoccupied lovers are anxious about losing their mates; they obsess over every little contretemps and can be really clingy. *Dismissing* people protect themselves from the pain of loss by not letting people get too close in the first place. *Fearful or avoidant* people crave close relationships but have difficulty trusting others. *Secure* people know they're loved, and feel confident about loving in return.

Marazziti wanted to assess how anxious the different types of people were about their attachments. Oxytocin is generally considered to be *anxiolytic*, that is, an anxiety reducer. Both preoccupied and fearful or avoidant people score high on anxiety in relationships. Dismissive people have limited their exposure to anxiety by refusing to allow anyone to matter too much.

After categorizing the subjects' attachment styles, the researchers sampled their blood for two months, measuring the amount of oxytocin in each sample. (Although the mechanisms that release oxytocin into the blood are different from those that release it into the nervous system, several studies support a correlation between the two. It's relatively easy to measure levels in blood, and researchers have come to accept that what's circulating in the blood reflects what's running through the nervous system.)

The Pisa team looked for links between the presence and duration of romantic attachments, the amount of anxiety a test subject felt about his or her lover, and the oxytocin level. Because oxytocin is the hormone of peace and satisfaction, you might expect that the more secure people would have the highest levels. Instead, the Pisans found that the more anxious someone was about romance, the more oxytocin circulated in her veins. The researchers think their study reveals a link between the state of anxiety that comes with romance and oxytocin.

But why would the anxious lover have higher oxytocin levels than the secure one? The study doesn't show whether it's a cause or a consequence of the anxiety, but the researchers think that the brains of the worried lovers may release extra oxytocin to counteract the stress caused by uncertainty and fear of rejection. (Another study showed elevated levels of oxytocin in the blood when both humans and prairie voles were isolated or stressed [Grippo, Cushing, and Carter 2007].) Their hypothesis is that, for some of us, a romantic relationship is more stressful than comforting, so the body keeps boosting oxytocin so that we can overcome the fear of rejection or pain long enough to experience the pleasures of attachment. This mechanism may have evolved, they think, to allow our remote ancestors to overcome their instinctual avoidance of strangers in order to meet, mate, and reproduce.

As they wrote in the paper presenting the study, "Humans are obliged to face a paradox which is fundamental to the survival of the species: they are attracted to, courted by, and breed with genetically unrelated individuals whom they would otherwise instinctively avoid" (Marazziti et al. 2006, 28).

Romance: The Next Level

So, what is this overpowering motivational drive that we know as romantic love? We all know it when we feel it, but can you "prove" that you're really in love? When Helen Fisher (2004) decided to find out, she first had to define it. That project alone took her a couple of years. To start, she and her team identified characteristics of the "truly, madly, deeply" state. They found thirteen aspects of romantic love that held true across cultures. Everyone believes the beloved is unique and can do no wrong. We all become emotionally dependent on the beloved, suffering wild mood swings depending on how he or she acts toward us. Sexual desire focuses on the beloved to the exclusion of others, but sex may not seem as important as the emotional intimacy. We can't stop thinking about the beloved, and begin to rebuild our lives around him or her. But Fisher found one other, telling quality of romantic love that cuts across all cultures: this crazy love can't last.

The Chemistry of Romance

Romance, as anyone can tell you, doesn't make us feel calm. Neither does it engage the attachment system. Instead, it revs up our competitive instincts. That's why it's not really accurate to lump together romance and love. When Fisher and colleagues (2002) scanned the brains of people who said they were intensely in love, it was the reward systems of their brains that were activated—*not* the connection system. The reward system is the seat of our most basic drives, the ones that impel us toward activities that will keep us alive, healthy, and propagating. It's what drove our ancestors up a tree to snag a juicy piece of fruit. It seems that romantic love isn't so much an emotion as a motivated state that pushes us to go after the prize of love (Aron et al. 2005).

The neurochemistry of romance, too, is different from that of lust or love. There's more to it than the push of testosterone and the pull of oxytocin. Fisher made some educated guesses about which neurochemicals were spiking this almost obsessive, addictive behavior. She homed in on dopamine, norepinephrine, and serotonin as the intoxicating ingredients (Fisher 2004).

Elevated levels of dopamine induce just the kinds of obsessive, excited behavior we feel when we're wildly in love. Dopamine creates the focused attention, hypervigilance, and energy that keep us intent on obtaining a reward. It can produce the euphoria that goes along with loss of appetite, sleeplessness, and manic energy—as well as the anxiety when a date goes bad.

High levels of norepinephrine help us learn faster in novel situations, remembering stimuli we haven't experienced before. So Fisher hypothesized that norepinephrine might contribute to that ability to remember every little thing he said or did. Rising levels of dopamine further stimulate the brain's reward center, creating the manic energy and obsessive attention to everything the beloved says or does. At the same time, it stimulates the wild elation that's the most magical part of new love (Fisher 2004).

Finally, that fixation that keeps the lover from thinking about her geometry test is not so different from the intrusive thinking experienced by people who suffer from obsessive-compulsive disorder. *Selective serotonin-reuptake inhibitors* like Prozac and Effexor relieve the symptoms of OCD by increasing the amount of serotonin in the brain. Therefore, Fisher thought, lowered serotonin might be the third element in the mix.

The Passionate Brain

Fisher wanted to look at the brains of people who were in the throes of romance, but first, she had to find them. She developed a questionnaire designed to determine just how much in love someone was. She gave the seventy-two-question test to groups of Americans and Japanese, and found that those who reported being madly in love were similar in both cultures. In fact, the essence of romantic love remained true regardless of gender, age, sexual orientation, religion, or ethnicity. When it comes to romance, we are truly equal. With this validation, she used the questionnaire to find test subjects willing to have their brains scanned.

Fisher teamed with neuroscientists Arthur Aron, Debra Mashek, Haifang Li, and Lucy Brown (2002) to watch neurons fire with longing and desire. They used fMRI to map the brain activity of seventeen love-besotted people (by their own reports) as they looked at photos of their beloveds. The fMRI images show active regions of the brain as bright spots. While most of the subjects did show some activity in the parts of the brain used to process emotions, it wasn't consistent. What was very consistent, however, was activation of the part of the brain that helps us mobilize to achieve goals or obtain a reward. The noggins of her love-crazed subjects glimmered with activity in the nucleus accumbens, a structure that's part of the reward center. The more passionate a person was about his or her lover, the more it lit up.

This explains why we're so willing to ditch responsibilities and blow off friends and family when we're newly in love. The brain system that normally would be concerned with the goal of getting a master's degree or finishing that big corporate presentation has been hijacked by the most pressing evolutionary goal of all: obtaining a mate who will help us pass on our genes.

Fisher's team found bursts of activity in another part of the brain, the ventral tegmental area, which is also an important part of the reward system. This area pumps out dopamine, distributing it to other areas of the brain to mobilize all the body's forces to grab that reward, in this case, the beloved. Notice that the researchers did *not* see the hypothalamus getting involved here. Romantic love is not about the bond of oxytocin.

Hooked on Passion

In fact, romance is much more like an addiction in terms of brain activity. Andreas Bartels and Semir Zeki (2000) of University College London found that romantic passion hijacks the rational brain as it wracks the body in its throes. Their research also illustrated the similarity between the high that's your brain on love and the rush of your brain on drugs. These research subjects had been in love for an average of 28.8 months, but they still reported being "deeply, madly" in love. Bartels and Zeki asked them to look at photos of good friends and photos of their romantic partners as their brains were scanned. When the lovers gazed at their beloveds, there was much higher activity in a few very specific regions of the brain than when they looked at their pals.

Like Fisher, Bartels and Zeki saw fireworks in the brain's reward system, specifically in the *caudate nucleus*, a mass of brain cells that's filled with dopamine receptors. (A malfunctioning caudate also is a prime suspect in obsessive-compulsive disorder, lending weight to Fisher's hypothesis about the relationship between OCD and romantic love.) Their imaging study homed in on the brain regions involved in making romance a full body-brain experience.

The first of these, the *insula*, connects the brain's emotional centers to the limbic system, thereby changing the body's physical state in response to its emotional one. It strongly responds to dopamine, and it's also implicated in addiction to things like cocaine, alcohol, and tobacco.

Lust, Romance, and Love

When you're gripped by passion, it can be confusing to sort out exactly how you feel. "Is this really love?" you ask yourself. While your emotions may be swirling together, lust, romance, and committed love release different neurochemicals and activate different parts of the brain. Here's the difference:

State	Sensations	Brain Structures	Neurochemicals
Lust	Arousal Engorgement Excitement	Right amygdala Anterior cingulate Ventral striatum Thalamus Hypothalamus (men)	Testosterone
Romance	Focused attention Obsession	Medial insula Anterior cingulate Caudate nucleus Putamen Ventral tegmental area Ventral pallidum	Dopamine Norepinephrine Low serotonin
Love	Calm Connection	Ventral pallidum Medial insula* Cingulate gyrus* Prefrontal cortex* Lateral orbitofrontal cortex*	Oxytocin Dopamine

* These brain regions are involved in maternal love; to date, no images have been made of the brains of people in long-term marriages.

The large *anterior cingulate cortex* takes part in both rational decision making and emotions, especially empathy and anticipation. This region pays close attention when any kind of reward comes into view.

At the same time, some of the brain systems involved in fear and depression were deactivated. Most notably, looking at photos of the loved one calmed down the amygdala, the seat of fear, sadness, and aggression.

Bartels and Zeki were surprised that activity was restricted to such a few, small patches of the brain. Their conclusion was that a unique network within the brain comes alive to evoke the state of romantic love. When they compared the lovers' fMRIs with brain scans of people who'd taken cocaine, they found the same pattern of brain activity.

How Sex Forges the Bond

Most people in the throes of romance want to merge with their beloveds by making love. Sex serves a different purpose in the romantic stage of a relationship than it does in a long-term, committed relationship. In this early stage, it reinforces what scientists call your "preference" for the other, a state we experience much more strongly. "Delight" or "ecstasy" would be a better word. Later, when the intoxicating neurochemicals of romance have ebbed, the oxytocin released during sex reinforces the bond and helps us weather the inevitable annoyances and hardships of living with someone and raising a family.

Sex is designed to feel so good—sometimes, better than anything else—so that we want to do it again and again, thereby perpetuating the species. Over time, it creates a bond between sex partners that keeps them committed to caring for each other and their children. The theory is that, during sex, the *hippocampus*, the brain area responsible for short-term memory, goes to work, remembering just who is responsible for all this excitement and fun. At orgasm, oxytocin stimulates social memory, tying the experience of physical pleasure to the person who shared it.

Because of the oxytocin release at orgasm, you could say that sex is the beginning of the end of romantic love and the beginning of the next phase: a deeper, oxytocin-based bond. But this transition doesn't happen overnight. At first, oxytocin is just an additional element in the heady mix of neurochemicals that makes romance so thrilling. You can expect to stay high on romance for a year or two before your levels of dopamine and serotonin return to normal (Marazziti et al. 1999). In the meantime, while oxytocin works its bonding magic, it's just as important for hot sex as it is for warm hugs. In fact, sex and love are deeply intertwined in our brains. Thanks to oxytocin, sex not only produces pleasure but also creates joy, a delight in the sex partner that becomes as addictive as heroin. So it's not surprising that oxytocin coursing through the bloodstream is necessary for sexual activity in men and women. While the neurochemistry of your relationship will change as time goes by, the neurochemistry of sex remains the same.

His and Her Arousal

A man's sexual excitement turns up the volume in the hypothalamus, the brain's oxytocin factory. During this arousal period, the hypothalamus releases oxytocin into the spinal cord, where it travels to the nerves that control erectile tissue. Far from being a woman thing, oxytocin is critical for getting the penis up (Argiolas and Melis 2004).

Experiments with rats show just how crucial it is for male sexual activity—and also how, even in these lowly rodents, sex starts in the brain. You can reliably create erections in a male rat by injecting oxytocin into its brain, whereas an injection into its bloodstream increases the number of ejaculations the rat can produce in a given period while reducing the resting time it needs between ejaculations (Pfaus and Everitt 2000). By the way, sildenafil, the drug sold as Viagra to help men with erectile dysfunction, also increases the amount of oxytocin released by the pituitary glands of rats (Jackson 2007).

There's no comparable research on women. We could speculate that, because the human female's genitals are analogous to the male's, their brain structures are the same, and their biochemistries are similar (except for the different levels of sex hormones), oxytocin is just as important for engorgement of the clitoris as it is for erection of the penis.

His and Her Orgasms

As we've seen, the sex hormones put a different sheen on the oxytocin effect; the difference extends to the way men and women orgasm. You can see this divergence reflected in brain-imaging studies. In 2003, Gert Holstege, head of the neuroanatomy program at the University of Groningen in Holland, was the first to scan the brains of men and women in the height of arousal (Holstege et al. 2003). He managed to make couples comfortable enough in the sterile, mechanical environment of a PET scanner that they could get excited and even orgasm while enduring an intravenous infusion of radioactive sugar water with a scientist standing by. PET, or *positron emission tomography*, shows which areas of the brain are more active, as indicated by their greater metabolism of glucose.

The person whose brain was being scanned lay very still on the bench, head inside the big magnetic ring, while his or her partner did all the work. It was tricky, because a PET scan measures brain activity for only a two-minute period. This is plenty of time when watching the brain do such tasks as looking at photos or remembering numbers, but that's a pretty narrow window for human sexual response (Holstege 2007).

Despite the obstacles, Holstege's team was able to record twenty-three orgasms among the eleven men (Holstege et al. 2003) and thirteen women (Georgiadis et al. 2006) in the two studies. They found huge variation in the way the brains of men and women functioned during orgasm. Both sexes experienced deactivation in the amygdala, the part of the brain responsible for assessing fear or danger. But this effect was much, much stronger in women. Their PET scans show hardly any activity at all in this area. While the men's amygdalae were also calmer, there were some areas that remained alert.

One of the effects of oxytocin is precisely this: reducing activity in the fight-or-flight coordinating amygdala. Although these studies weren't looking at oxytocin, we can speculate that this difference between sexes is due to the greater responsiveness of the female brain to oxytocin.

These researchers also found increased activation in both the men's and women's reward circuits, but the men's activation was much greater. This needs confirmation by further studies. But together, these results seem to fit with some cultural stereotypes: men find sex rewarding in itself, while women respond as much to the relationship as to the sex itself. This explains why it often seems as if a woman is eager to commit long before a man is. Nevertheless, men are subject to the same addictive properties of sex, and their neurochemistries are also primed to bond with their lovers.

Balancing the Differences

It's no surprise that we men and women often feel as if we're from different planets, as John Gray has pointed out (see *Men Are from Mars, Women Are from Venus*, HarperCollins, 1992). And sometimes, it seems amazing that we can get together at all. Of course, when we fall in love, suddenly those differences seem to fall away; we feel merged into a single being. That sense of union we experience in a new romance may be the result of lovers' neurochemical profiles becoming more alike.

In a 2004 study of twenty-four people who were newly in love, Donatella Marazziti and Domenico Canale of the University of Pisa found that the couples' hormone levels adjusted themselves to make each of them more like the other. The testosterone levels of the men were lower than normal, while the women's were a bit higher. The lovers' cortisol levels also were significantly higher than normal. All hormone levels returned to normal in one to two years—the semi-official "romance is over" deadline.

The Oxytocin Flood

As the hypothalamus reacts to sexual excitement by flooding the brain and spinal cord with oxytocin, it signals the pituitary gland to pump more of it into the bloodstream. Sex is an unusual state, neurochemically speaking, because the same substance—oxytocin—is going into the brain and into the blood at the same time, creating a coordinated, whole-body effect.

The oxytocin level in the bloodstream gradually builds as both men and women become aroused, and both sexes experience a rush of oxytocin when they orgasm (Murphy et al. 1987). When he ejaculates, a burst of oxytocin through his arteries stimulates the contractions that eject sperm (Thackare, Nicholson, and Whittington 2006).

This chemical flood may also cause the contractions of the vagina that are associated with climax. These contractions make the orgasm more intense, in an endocrine feedback loop: stimulating the genitals causes the release of oxytocin into the bloodstream. The oxytocin then intensifies the contractions even more (Komisaruk, Beyer-Flores, and Whipple 2006). In an example of the way nature likes to be thrifty, the gush of oxytocin during a woman's climax also speeds sperm up the fallopian tubes. Oxytocin causes the same kind of rhythmic contractions in the uterus during sex that it does during labor—and those little contractions tend to push the sperm toward the ovary with the ripest egg. This is because the dominant follicle—the one with an egg that's ready for fertilization—sends out more estrogen than the other side. This estrogen output peaks right before ovulation. Because estrogen enhances the effects of oxytocin, the fallopian tube on the dominant side contracts a little more, propelling sperm to the place it's likely to do the most good—in terms of perpetuating the human race, at any rate. So, it seems, the better the sex, the more oxytocin is released, and the more likely a woman might be to get pregnant (Kunz et al. 2007).

Sex and Reward

In any case, we're all the same in one way: orgasm is a highly rewarding, full-brain experience. Dopamine pathways in the brain's reward center are on fire during ejaculation in men and during orgasm in women. The nucleus accumbens, that key part of the brain's reward circuitry, tingles during orgasm just as it would if you experienced a cocaine rush.

The pleasure of sex is evolution's way of making sure animals procreate as much as possible. The combination of dopamine and oxytocin is evolution's way of giving the tender human infant the best possible shot at survival: two parents cooperating to keep him safe and healthy (Kendrick 2000).

Remember, oxytocin calms the amygdala and creates feelings of trust. During sex and orgasm, the right half of the amygdala seems to play the same role that it does in the rest of our lives (Beauregard,

Lévesque, and Bourgouin 2001). The right hemisphere is especially important for creating the kinds of emotional memories that stay below the level of conscious thought, so the right amygdala is thought to be more involved in positive feelings, while the left amygdala handles the darker emotions. During lovemaking, the right amygdala probably assigns emotional tone to the feelings of orgasm and acts as a central switching station for the bombardment of sensory signals coming from the skin and genital organs (Komisaruk and Whipple 2005). So, as you make love, you're unconsciously building a library of good feelings that your amygdala associates with your beloved. As this library of delight grows larger, simply looking into each other's eyes—even seeing your beloved across a crowded room—makes you feel happy.

Good-Bye to Romance?

In modern society, the hormonal rush of romance may indeed be an important step in mate seeking, helping us to somehow narrow down the hundreds of people we come into contact with each day and pay attention to one likely lovemate. But romance all too often brings heartbreak and disappointment. Why bother?

In fact, you don't need to go through the romantic stage to find true love. To see just how much of an invention romance is, look at any society that employs the ancient practice of arranged marriage.

Certainly, such marriages can be overly pragmatic, when the goal is to solidify business interests or political alliances. But most parents combine pragmatism with hope when looking for a mate for their child. They seek out other families that are like themselves in the ways that matter: values, education, and social position. These are the things that seem totally irrelevant when you're young and in love, but they can drive a couple apart when they try to build a life together. At best, arranged marriages are stabilized by tradition and the support of the larger families and society as a whole. "Love will come," they assure their children. And it often does.

Sex, sleeping together, being together in the home, and then perhaps the coming of children all wrap the couple in an oxytocin bond, thanks to that unique tie between oxytocin and reward in our brains. Oxytocin keeps you bonded enough to endure the years it takes to raise a squirming, crying infant into a strong adult who's ready to carry the family genes into the future.

Why Can't I Fall in Love?

If our brains evolved to form a bond with a mate, if our neurochemistries respond to romance as though it were an addictive drug, if the oxytocin and dopamine released during sex and orgasm reinforce the desire for the sex partner, why doesn't this always work? Some of us blithely—or desperately—move from one sexual encounter to the next without experiencing that deeper connection. Or we never feel that spark of desire and hope that lets us leap into the unknown of another human heart. Why? Why not?

We saw in chapter 2 how babies are born without a developed oxytocin response; each of us must learn to love from the person who takes care of us. Not everyone gets the right kind of mothering to help his or her brain learn to release oxytocin in times of physical and emotional intimacy. And we saw in chapter 3 how, as we grow through adolescence, we tend to choose the kinds of relationships that mirror that early lack. When we go out into the world and begin to form adult-style relationships that include dating, sex, and possibly cohabitation, we bring whatever emotional or, rather, neurochemical abilities or disabilities we have to our romances.

While oxytocin is part of the physiological experience of orgasm, your brain may not have developed strong and healthy oxytocin receptors in the area that keeps track of social relationships. Therefore, sex for you may not reinforce a preference for your sex partners. Genetics likely plays a role here. In the monogamous prairie vole, Liz Hammock and Larry Young of Emory University, along with their colleagues (2005), found a variation in the gene that controls the receptor for vasopressin, a neurochemical that's very similar to oxytocin and is also related to bonding. Male prairie voles with some variations in this gene don't form monogamous pair-bonds at all (Hammock and Young 2005)—and the human version of this gene has similar variations. Now, remember epigenetic influences, the way the environment helps determine whether genes are switched on or off? Certain combinations of a genetic variation and early mothering style could lead to an inability to bond via sex. You could enjoy sex immensely without feeling the strong stirrings of affection and connection that normally accompany it.

The science of romance is less clear. Helen Fisher thinks that the same variations in vasopressin and oxytocin activity in the brain's reward center and in the *ventral pallidum*, a structure that's more active in long-term relationships, could also account for differences in "partner preference," the early stage of courtship in which we identify that special someone we hope to make our own (Fisher, Aron, and Brown 2006). If these brain structures are less responsive to oxytocin, vasopressin, and dopamine, you might feel lust and attraction without that exciting spark of romance.

But don't despair. This doesn't mean that our genes determine whether or not we'll be able to fall in love and stay in love. As we saw in chapter 3, your brain has the ability to change its ways at any time. If you're stuck at the sex or romance stage of relationships, you can use the tools in chapter 3 to learn to fall into deep, committed love for good. In the next chapters, we'll take a look at the chemistry of committed love, and learn how to raise a new generation of children who touch, connect, and love.

Addicted to Romance?

Romance is exciting, fun—and almost literally addictive. No wonder. It fires up the same rewarding brain circuits that cocaine does. But, if you're hooked on romance, you may never learn to move on to the next stage: committed, oxytocin-based love. Use these strategies to keep your head above the fog of passion:

If you're not in a relationship: Aside from sex, romantic relationships fulfill many of our most basic needs for human contact, while the hurry of modern life provides fewer opportunities for other kinds of connection. Instead of focusing on romance, put more energy into establishing or nurturing other kinds of relationships. Make a standing date to meet friends for drinks or dinner. Join a sports league, a club, or a church—and show up religiously.

If you're in a new relationship: Slow it down now. Enjoy this exciting stage to the fullest without pushing for sex or commitment. You may feel, "This is it!" Remind yourself that this feeling could change. Set a goal for how long you want to date before having sex. If you're looking for a long-term relationship, waiting six months will give you time to assess the chances. Sharing that goal with your partner is a good way to build trust—or to find out that he or she isn't so understanding. If you just want to have fun, waiting at least a month will give you a sense of whether or not you're dating a creep.

If you're in an established relationship: The excitement of romance inevitably wears off. After a year or two of steady and relatively happy togetherness, levels of dopamine and serotonin in the brain return to normal. This is the point at which too many people say, "I just don't love you anymore." What they mean is, "I don't feel that romantic high anymore." People who are addicted to romance may at this point engineer a breakup or introduce drama into their lives to recreate the ups and downs of early-stage love.

If your oxytocin response is strong, and you have a sexual relationship that leads to orgasm, you will have developed an oxytocin bond with your partner by this time. In this case, breaking your addiction to romance means accepting that your relationship is in a different stage. Understand that you've moved from being in love to loving. Talk about your life goals with your partner, and decide where you want to go next. Find a new kind of excitement in getting married, shopping for a house, planning to have a baby, or starting a business together.

If your oxytocin response is weak, you can get stuck in a perpetual cycle of romantic boom and bust. You seem to inevitably lose interest at a certain point. You have two choices: take a break from romance and focus on building your oxytocin response through other kinds of connection, as described throughout this book, or work on building a bond using the Attachment Dance exercise from chapter 3.

If your oxytocin response is only activated in response to angry, cold, or abusive people, you may stay muddled in romance for years. That's because the conflict in such a relationship keeps you in the anxious early stage. These relationships are extremely hard to end. But the excitement of never knowing what's next—and never getting what you really need—is hard on your body and your emotions. This kind of relationship also activates the brain systems of addiction, and it may help to use the tools people employ to break other kinds of addiction, including psychotherapy and support groups.

Chapter 5

the chemistry of commitment

ah, courtship: A northern harrier hawk repeatedly climbs the sky and then plunges toward the earth, enticing his desired partner to join him in this expression of untrammeled power. The humpback whale casts his mysterious and ever-changing song through miles of pelagic water, hoping it will be heard somewhere in the deep. A teenage boy anoints himself with a potent mix of styrene-acrylates copolymer, hydrofluoro-carbon, and fragrance (also known as body spray) before he heads to the mall.

The Monogamous Brain

We humans have the most highly developed brains on the planet. Yet, when it comes to sexual attraction and mate seeking, we're no different from our butt-sniffing mammalian cousins. Our passions are ruled by the same neurochemicals that govern the hawk and the whale.

But love—that's a different story. Fundamentally, we're made for deep, lifelong love for one mate. We humans are among just 3 percent or so of mammals that seem to be hardwired for monogamy. This small set of monogamous mammals—including the prairie vole, the titi monkey, and the fat-tailed dwarf lemur—have a unique receptivity to oxytocin, the brain chemical that enables us to form the bond we know as love.

The Coolidge Effect

Most male animals mate early and often, with as many partners as possible. This system has reproductive advantage for the male of the species: the more eggs he can fertilize, the better the chances that some of his offspring will live to reproduce themselves, passing along his genes.

There's a famous and probably apocryphal story about President Calvin Coolidge and his wife, Grace Anna. As the tale goes, the Coolidges visit a farm, where, on separate tours, they're each impressed by the amorous prowess of the top rooster. Mrs. Coolidge and her guide pause by the chicken coop, and she asks him how often the rooster copulates.

"Dozens of times a day," she's told.

"Well," she says, "please tell that to Mr. Coolidge."

Mr. Coolidge is duly told and, after a moment of dismay, he asks, "The same hen every time?"

"Oh, no, Mr. President. A different hen every time."

"Well," he says, "you tell *that* to Mrs. Coolidge."

Psychologists G. Bermant and D. F. Lott used this anecdote to explain a phenomenon they'd observed: a male rat who'd copulated to exhaustion with one particular female could somehow manage to "get it up" and begin all over again when presented with a different female rat in heat (Bermant, Lott, and Anderson 1968). The Coolidge effect is reliable not only in rats but also in most other mammals. Ranchers know that a bull will refuse to copulate again with a cow he's already mounted, no matter how they try to disguise her. When he's done, she's done.

Some women may swear that modern men experience the Coolidge effect. But a man is not a rat, hamster, or bull. While the brains of those creatures impel the males to spread their semen as widely as possible, the brain of the human male, like that of the human female, drives him to pin his desires on one particular woman. Each time he makes love, his orgasm teaches his brain that *she*, this particular woman out of all the other lovelies, is the source of pleasure and comfort. He can make love to her day after day after day, until their grandkids present them with a gold-plated cookie platter.

Monogamy has its own adaptive advantages. Instead of expending all their energy in mate seeking—and exposing themselves to danger from rivals and predators—monogamous male mammals cohabit with their mates and make a fairly equal contribution to child rearing by gathering food, defending the nest, and making sure the offspring don't wander away. (In fact, some males do more to raise the young than the female does.) His investment in the offspring increases the likelihood that babies will grow up and carry on his genes, bettering his reproductive odds just as much as the sperm-scattering approach does. It's also a better deal for the female; her mate's protection and help make it more likely that she'll survive the perils of pregnancy, birth, and nursing.

Love in the Brain

Whether a species is monogamous seems to depend on a small variation in the distribution of oxytocin and dopamine receptors in the brain. Most mammals, male and female, monogamous or not, have remarkably similar brain structures and neurochemistry. Their brains produce oxytocin, as well as vasopressin, a closely related molecule that seems to stimulate protective behaviors (Bales 2007). Dopamine, the chemical messenger responsible for feelings of pleasure, drives them all to go after the rewards of food and sex. And cortisol puts them on alert for danger.

What's different about the monogamous minority is the way their brains seem to be set up to pair the rewarding dopamine rush with oxytocin, the neurochemical of social connection. The peculiar placement of oxytocin receptors in human brains—and in those of the rest of the monogamous 3 percent—ties social attachment to the brain's powerful reward structures. The key to whether an animal will mate for life or run from one partner to the next seems to be where receptors for those neurotransmitters are located (Young and Wang 2004). In monogamous brains, the reward centers are rich with receptors for not only dopamine but also oxytocin, the molecule of bonding. The same systems involved in addiction to drugs lead us humans to form a benign addiction to our mates, families, and friends.

So, in the nonmonogamous brain, sex feels really good, while in the monogamous brain, the quick, intense reward of sex is tied to a particular sex partner, creating a conditioned response that's not much different from the addicting high of cocaine or methamphetamine (Young and Wang 2004). The combined chemical message says, "Sex felt really good with *you*. Let's do it some more."

Social Monogamy

Evolution may have hijacked the brain's attachment circuits in aid of monogamous love, because raising those extremely weak and defenseless human children in pairs provides adaptive advantages. In prehistoric times (and even today) children were more likely to survive to pass on their parents' genes in a dual-parent family.

But the woman and children's need for support conflicts with the sexual promiscuity that, in most species, creates reproductive success for the male. Monogamy helps resolve the conflict. A man who lives with his mate and has sex with her frequently is more likely to be the biological father of the offspring he's investing in. In primitive times, the male half of the pair could protect his woman and children from animal and human predators, and he could provide food when pregnancy, labor, or sickness kept her lying in. Those adaptive advantages seem to remain in our modern times. The largest predictors of divorce in the twentieth century were infidelity and infertility (Fraley and Shaver 2000).

This is not to say that men—and women, too—are so hardwired for monogamy that infidelity is impossible or even difficult. Obviously, sex outside of marriage is always just a phone call away. We humans, like most monogamous mammals, engage in what biologists call "social monogamy," defined as living with one partner to whom we're bonded, sharing the work of maintaining a home and raising children, with the occasional sexual adventure. In fact, there may be no such thing as true sexual monogamy anywhere in the animal kingdom.

Scientists can estimate how often couples in a monogamous species copulate with other individuals by doing DNA tests on the young. The results show that monogamy is more of a social system than a sexual one. Researchers who've examined the DNA of monogamous birds in Europe have found that between 29 and 68 percent of the offspring are the result of "extra-pair copulation" (Kempenaers et. al 1992).

We don't seem to have any comparable stats for human paternity—talk about a hot potato! But there are anecdotal reports from surgeons who do organ transplants or bone marrow transfusions. In these cases, doctors look first to parents or siblings as donors, because they share genetic material. However, in many more cases than they expect, when they do the DNA test, it turns out not to be a match: the father of the family wasn't the biological father of a daughter, or the brother and sister are really half siblings. It seems that modern humans are just as likely to hedge their genetic bets with some extra-pair copulation.

Love Among the Voles

Much of what we know about monogamy we learned from the prairie vole. These humble dirt-colored beasts have a family life every bit as stable as the Bradys'. Prairie voles, or *Microtus ochrogaster*, as they're officially named, just love to be together.

Thomas Insel, now director of the National Institutes of Health, took the first step toward figuring out just how that monogamous 3 percent gets that way by comparing the sociable prairie vole with its close cousin, *Microtus montanus*, the montane vole (Witt, Carter, and Insel 1991).

Montane voles look and act a lot like their prairie-dwelling relatives except when it comes to mating. Instead of forming a lifelong family huddle, they live alone in an isolated burrow, socializing only long enough to copulate. The males show no interest in their offspring, and the females are unenthusiastic mothers, sometimes abandoning their litters before they're able to fend for themselves. Even the pups don't seem to crave maternal care; by five days old, they show little distress when removed from their mothers.

Following up on a suggestion by Diane Witt that differences between prairie and montane voles could be due to the pattern of oxy-

tocin receptors in their brains, Insel tried blocking the oxytocin receptors in female prairie voles (Witt, Carter, and Insel 1991). A female that
couldn't respond to oxytocin behaved like a montane vole: she would
mate normally but then show no further interest in her partner.

rodent dating

Sue Carter has a library of voles. Next to her lab on the Chicago
campus of the University of Illinois, there's a room holding shelf after
shelf of plastic bins, each with a family of prairie voles huddled happily
together.

Carter, a professor of psychiatry and head of the university's Brain-
Body Center, made international headlines in the early 1990s when she
helped discover that oxytocin was the key to the female prairie voles'
bond. As a biologist at the University of Maryland, she'd been studying estrogen's role in sexual behavior. Following up on studies showing
that oxytocin helped create the bond between a ewe and her lamb,
she began experimenting with oxytocin and prairie voles to see how it
affected their social behavior.

By 1995, she had created a theoretical model of how oxytocin
facilitated the forming of bonds when these little creatures mated. Her
theory was that interactions between oxytocin, vasopressin, and glucocorticoids—the steroid hormones produced by the adrenal gland—were
involved in the bond between prairie vole couples, as well as in the
male's parental behavior (Carter, DeVries, and Getz 1995). In one of the
most definitive experiments, Carter and her team looked at the effects
of oxytocin in both male and female prairie voles (Williams, Catania,
and Carter 1992). Injecting oxytocin directly into the brains of males
and females increased their desire for contact, and it also increased
their preference for their partners.

To emphasize that this was the effect of the injections, Carter
and her collaborators also injected the prairie voles with oxytocin or
vasopressin antagonists, chemicals that prevent receptors from binding
with a chemical (Cho et al. 1999). Blocking the effects of either oxytocin or vasopressin reduced an animal's desire for social contact of any
kind. These experiments showed that either oxytocin or vasopressin
increased socializing, while the bond between mates may depend on

both oxytocin and vasopressin. A later experiment by Carter and Karen Bales revealed that a single injection of oxytocin at birth made an adult male prairie vole bond with its mate faster (Bales and Carter 2003).

In another experiment, Carter and Bruce Cushing gave subcutaneous injections of oxytocin to virgin female prairie voles for five days before placing each with a sexually experienced male (Cushing and Carter 1999). Usually, naive (in the sexual sense) female prairie voles need to spend about twenty-four hours in the presence of an unrelated male before they come into heat. In Carter and Cushing's experiments, the females that had been primed with oxytocin were much more likely to mate during the first two days of male contact than were an untreated group.

Let's be anthropomorphic: you could think of this as rodent dating. The juvenile female voles have spent their whole lives so far in the family nest. Like most mammals, they fear unfamiliar individuals. Having social contact not only removes that fear but also brings on estrus when the female's system recognizes that this male is both safe and available. The injection of oxytocin mimics that twenty-four-hour "dating" period that female voles in the wild need before they feel safe enough to mate with a strange male.

In a follow-up test, they split naive females into three groups. The control group received only saline solution. One group received estrogen, a tactic for increasing the female's willingness to mate. A third received oxytocin for five days, as in the previous experiment, and then a shot of estrogen. The combination of estrogen and oxytocin made those females readier to mate than estrogen alone or saline, the control treatment.

These experiments supported Carter's hypothesis that oxytocin was involved in social contact; the oxytocin injections seemed to produce the same effects as that of hanging out in proximity to an unfamiliar male vole. They also illustrated the way estrogen enhances the effects of oxytocin in the voles.

social memory

So, a vole meets a vole and remembers it. So what? Certainly, you can't bond with someone if you can't remember him. But you don't bond with everyone you remember meeting, and even among those you do bond with, there's a big difference in the degrees of warmth you feel for a pal and a lover. What makes one kind of affection warmer than another?

Zuoxin Wang, a professor at Florida State University and frequent collaborator with Insel, has homed in on the role of dopamine in bonding (Liu and Wang 2003). It seems to be the combination of dopamine's reward with oxytocin- or vasopressin-produced social memory that creates that monogamous bond in prairie voles.

Under Wang's leadership, one of his lab members, Brandon Aragona, and other researchers (Aragona et al. 2003) showed how dopamine is released in the nucleus accumbens, the reward center, of the prairie vole during mating. In their little brains, dopamine interacts with oxytocin to create the pair-bond. Later, Aragona showed more details of how dopamine creates a monogamous bond between prairie voles after a single mating session (Aragona et al. 2006). A particular form of dopamine, known as $D2$, acts on the reward system, making copulation with that individual rewarding. At the same time, a different form of dopamine, $D1$, acts on different receptors to promote the flip side of monogamy: rejecting unfamiliar females.

This work also illustrates how mating actually changes the structure of the male's brain. Mating reorganizes the nucleus accumbens and makes it more sensitive to D1, the dopamine that incites aggression against unfamiliar females. In other words, not only does the male's reward center get stimulated by dopamine when he's with his mate, he also becomes more faithful to her.

A Man or a Vole?

That's all very well, you say. But how do we know that a person is more like a prairie vole than a montane vole? While the oxytocin in prairie voles and humans is identical, and the two species share some similar brain structures, it's a long leap from a rodent to a person. The titi monkey, a football-sized ball of fur with a luxuriant silver tail, may provide the missing link between the monogamous prairie vole and human love.

A captive-bred colony of sixty titis, three generations, lives in a skylit metal building at the California National Primate Research Center, located at the University of California in Davis. They're not the most deluxe digs, but as a whole, the Primate Research Center is pretty low-key, just a nondescript stucco building set on several lush acres, surrounded by walnut orchards and hay fields in this small central California farming community.

Each titi family, the product of a "marriage" arranged by the biologists, spends most of its time shoulder to shoulder on perches in its cage. Those silver tails tend to twine around each other in a pendulous furry love knot. Titi monkeys are monogamous, and housing families in separate cages eliminates any extra-pair sexual activity. Mother, father, and juveniles usually cohabitate happily, although a few unlucky males may be removed for bad behavior. These guys live in solitary cages until a young female grows up enough to help one of them start a new family.

Karen Bales, mentioned earlier, was a protégée of Sue Carter who has taken Carter's monogamy studies up the evolutionary chain from vole to monkey. She and her colleagues at the University of California at Davis looked at the brains of titi males with the aim of finding differences between males in long-term relationships, those who had just formed a pair-bond, and those who hadn't mated (Bales et al. 2007b). They used PET scans and structural MRI to see how much glucose was being used by different areas of the animals' brains. In theory, the more glucose that's taken up by cells, the more active that region is.

The male monkeys with mates showed the same patterns of activity that the mated male voles did: higher activity in the reward circuits, as well as in areas of the brain that produce or respond to oxytocin or vasopressin. In other words, there seem to be some basic similarities in the way that a pair of voles and a pair of titi monkeys bond. It's still a leap from monkeys to humans, but the chasm is a lot narrower than it was before this study.

Men and Women *Are* Different

This book is about oxytocin, the chemical of empathy, trust, and love. But there's a joker in the deck: vasopressin. This somewhat mysterious chemical differs from oxytocin by just two amino acids; both chemicals

99

probably evolved from a single precursor in the days when our ancestors slithered. Researchers haven't quite figured out what vasopressin's role is, but it may be the key to some of the most confounding differences in the way that men and women lust and love.

Vasopressin is much harder to study in humans than oxytocin for three reasons. First, the level in a person's bloodstream doesn't correlate as well with levels in the nervous system, so researchers can't rely on taking blood samples to understand what's going on in the brain. Second, scientists have identified three different types of vasopressin receptors in humans, the same as in prairie voles. Third, you can't find people willing to take part in studies where vasopressin, or anything else, is injected into their brains (Carter 2007b).

Studies of rodents, including mice, rats, and voles, indicate that vasopressin may alter a male's bond with its mate. Scientists used to think that vasopressin regulates male monogamy the same way oxytocin does for the female. But Karen Bales and her colleagues (2004) have done experiments showing that it's oxytocin that's key for both male and female bonding. When Bales injected the brains of male prairie voles with a substance to block the effects of vasopressin, it had no effect on their bonds with their mates. After a period of separation, males whose vasopressin had been blocked scurried just as eagerly back to their chosen companions. In another experiment, Bales (Bales and Carter 2003) gave male prairie voles a single dose of an oxytocin blocker soon after they were born. When these males grew up, they failed to bond with a mate. They also displayed a lot less of the parental caring behavior typical of this species: they spent less time "huddling" with the pups, licked and groomed them less, and weren't as apt to retrieve babies that wandered out of the nest. These experiments show that oxytocin is a critical component of a male's bonding, as well as a female's.

But vasopressin does play a bigger role in stimulating fatherly behavior in male prairie voles than in females. In prairie voles, and other species of monogamous mammals, males will fight to protect the family and venture out to retrieve wandering pups. In these males, oxytocin is more related to the behavior of huddling up close with mother and pups in the nest, while vasopressin is more related to the "manly" traits of protecting the nest and keeping the kids in line.

The Protector Role

In humans, vasopressin is primarily produced in the hypothalamus, although the amygdala produces some as well. There's little difference between men and women in receptor distribution in these parts of the brain. But, just as oxytocin is amplified by estrogen, vasopressin is dependent on androgens, so males are more sensitive to it than females. Just like oxytocin, vasopressin is released into the bloodstream of men and women during sexual activity and intercourse. In a man, vasopressin peaks when he becomes fully aroused; oxytocin peaks with ejaculation. Women don't seem to experience this vasopressin peak, but this question needs more research (Carter 2007a).

One experiment points to the same influence of vasopressin on protective behaviors in humans as in voles: it seemed to put men on aggressive alert. In a study at Bowdoin College, psychologists gave men and women a whiff of vasopressin and then showed them photos of faces with carefully neutral expressions. The men who had sniffed vasopressin frowned more, and tended to see the neutral facial expressions in photos of men as unfriendly. When the women in the study looked at photos of other women, on the other hand, their facial muscle moved more often into friendly expressions, and they rated the strange women's photos as more friendly (Thompson et al. 2006).

The effects of this chemical may be very different for men and women, because while men and women have similar structures in the hypothalamus that release vasopressin into the nervous system, it's also produced in another part of the brain, one that's strongly influenced by male hormones: the *stria terminalis*. The stria terminalis is a band of nervous tissue connecting the amygdala to the hypothalamus.

The male amygdala and stria terminalis both have many more vasopressin-producing cells than a woman's, as well as more vasopressin receptors. That's because production of vasopressin in these areas is dependent on testosterone. Differences in the size of this band of nerves begin to appear during gestation, when the Y chromosome of the male fetus stimulates his mother's body to produce his first testosterone bath. This structure begins to grow again at puberty, with a second surge of testosterone. At maturity, a man's stria terminalis will be, on average, 39 percent larger than a woman's (Chung, De Vries, and Swaab 2002).

So, let's take another speculative leap here and assume that humankind *does* bond like the vole and the titi monkey. If so, it would provide a biological explanation for the perplexing mismatch between male and female romantic strategies. In human males, the drive to be the defenders of home and family may be as innate as it is in our mammal cousins.

Love: His and Hers

Have you ever heard a woman say that she feels love for someone deep in her womb? That could be those uterine oxytocin receptors sending out a message. Her body, primed for childbirth and coursing with estrogen, is extremely susceptible to the bonding influence of oxytocin. This is why she may begin to feel so attached, even before sex. If all it takes is a little canoodling to get the settle-down hormone flowing through her veins, when she makes love she feels she's in the arms of Mr. Right. Oxytocin makes her want to snuggle up for the night—and forever. The quiet times a woman craves with her man—gazing into his eyes, talking about feelings—are activities that boost oxytocin and make her feel bonded. And, romance for a woman tends to involve elements that, really, relate to nesting: dim lighting, flowers, and music—all help create the civilized equivalent of a warm, safe place to give birth.

But men fall more under the influence of vasopressin, so his romantic needs are quite different from hers. Excitement, danger, and the impetus to protect his woman are what make him feel bonded. All the mushy stuff that she needs seems boring and even a bit of a turnoff. The movie cliché where the hero saves a woman from peril, looks into her eyes, and passionately kisses her expresses an evolutionary truth. The testosterone and vasopressin in a man's system may keep him from turning into a cuddle bug. Instead, he's more likely to play the role of protector and warrior. That charge of testosterone and vasopressin may be the reason that after sex, while she wants to cuddle, he feels the urge to jump up and fix the car.

Once he's mated, vasopressin readies him to respond to challenge by amping up his sympathetic nervous system. In a challenge, vasopressin overrules the effect of oxytocin, turning off trust and friendly behavior.

Meanwhile, testosterone increases his energy and self-confidence, making him more willing to be aggressive. The man's tendency to be the disciplinarian of the family may have evolved into a social norm because it's such a comfortable part of his biology.

That twist that vasopressin gives to the male brain goes a long way toward explaining how differences between mothering and fathering might have come to be. A woman, as the sole provider of milk for babies, needs to be still to let them nurse. They have a better chance of surviving if she stays close to them, even in times of danger. The best defense may be to keep quiet and hope she isn't seen. Calming oxytocin activates her parasympathetic nervous system and helps her stay put. Once a man has impregnated his mate, he's more expendable. If he dies or is injured while fighting off a predator, he's nevertheless given the rest of the family a better shot at survival.

Translate this to modern humans and you get the stereotypes: Mommy is warm and nurturing, happy to putter around the house, and glad to settle in for a long chat. Daddy is striding out of the house to work and jumping up in the dark to investigate things that go bump in the night.

At the same time, the married (or mated) man's roaming instincts will be at least somewhat quelled as the sweet influence of oxytocin predominates over the rangy persuasions of testosterone. In fact, Peter Gray of the University of Nevada has found that testosterone levels in married men are actually lower than those of bachelors, making them more committed to the wife and kids. This held true across cultures. Gray's hypothesis is that this reflects a shift in the man's reproductive strategy, as he moves from sperm-scattering to investing in his family (Gray et al. 2004). He and his colleagues have yet to determine whether mated men have lower testosterone levels because they're in relationships or whether men with lower testosterone levels are more likely to settle down with a family. In either case, the lower levels of testosterone in these family men allow for a fuller flowering of the oxytocin response.

Lower testosterone and more oxytocin could make for mellower sex as well, and the oxytocin effect is probably what makes sex in a long-term relationship so different from those intense encounters during the early days of courtship or marriage. The nucleus accumbens, the brain system that keeps us focused on winning rewards, doesn't need to go into high gear when that reward is lying in bed next to us every night. Her body and brain, bathed in the calming effects of oxytocin, over time may tend to favor comfort over passion. He, too, is calmer and less excitable, which, overall, is a healthy state for him, even if he's less of a raging bull when it comes to sex.

The Marriage Benefit

Whether or not you engage in extra-pair copulation, it seems to be the oxytocin bond, not the sex, that matters. Numerous studies have found that, once they reach their fifties, married men are healthier and live longer than their single or divorced brethren (Kiecolt-Glaser and Newton 2001). Oxytocin's dual role, of physiological peacemaker and interpersonal bonder, is the reason. Just ten minutes of warm contact raises blood levels of oxytocin in both men and women, while lowering blood pressure and the stress hormone norepinephrine (Grewen et al. 2005). While the stress-buffering effects of oxytocin may be stronger in women, men get the same benefits—and those benefits last throughout the day, helping both cope with stress on the job.

A 2005 study led by Karen Grewen of the University of North Carolina scanned the brains of married women as they were threatened with receiving an electrical shock (Grewen et al. 2005). The women were divided into three groups: one group held their husbands' hands, one group held the hand of a male stranger, and the third group got no hand-holding whatsoever.

The brains of the women who held their mates' hands showed much less of a threat response than the other two groups, although holding a stranger's hand did provide at least some stress relief. What was most striking about the results of the study was that the better the marriage, the calmer the woman was in response to the threat.

Oxytocin also keeps a lid on marital spats, letting couples work out problems without getting enraged. In a 2008 study led by Beate Ditzen at Emory University, fifty couples were given either an oxytocin nasal spray or a placebo spray, and then asked to revisit a sore point in their relationships (Ditzen 2008). Their mock arguments were videotaped and scored, and researchers measured the heart rate and the level of cortisol, the stress hormone, in the couples' saliva. After arguing for ten minutes, everyone rated his or her own stress levels, and both groups felt about the same amount of tension; the people who inhaled oxytocin didn't feel any less stressed than the control group. But cortisol levels were significantly lower in the oxytocin group.

Psychologists who rated the couples' interactions based on body language, verbal expression, and tone of voice thought couples in the oxytocin group handled the interaction better: they were better able to articulate both negative and positive feelings, and they opened up to each other more than the other group did. Being able to handle conflict without tweaking makes it easier to collaborate with your mate, maintain your relationship, and thereby preserve the family—and pass along those genes.

Over time, married folk become more resilient and permanently less stressed out. Happy couples enter a virtuous circle: oxytocin makes them feel closer, and the closer they feel, the more oxytocin they produce. Flushed with oxytocin, each person reinforces the comfort and support the other provides (Grewen, Girdler, and Light 2005). At the same time, oxytocin traveling through their bloodstreams keeps their immune systems tuned up, improves their ability to heal, and helps them get the rest and physical relaxation they need to keep their bodies strong. This intertwining of emotional connection—love—and physical health explains the depth of our need for intimacy.

You may not choose traditional marriage or sexual monogamy. But, as this chapter has shown, we all have an innate need for oxytocin-based relationships that are very different from romantic desire. You may find such a relationship not only with a mate but also with a best friend, a mentor, a parent, or your own child. In the next chapter, we'll take a look at how you can parent in a way that builds your bond with your children and helps them maintain a healthy oxytocin response.

Gay and Lesbian Mating

What makes a person homosexual is a mystery still to be revealed—as well as a sociopolitical hot potato. But let's boldly talk about what the oxytocin hypothesis might mean for same-sex relationships.

Certainly, gay men and lesbian women love and bond the same way as straight people do. Their hypothalami produce the same spurts of oxytocin and vasopressin, and they enjoy the same exciting rushes of dopamine. Sex creates the same association in the brain's reward system between a sex partner and feeling great, inscribing a social memory that causes one person to prefer another.

In gay love, however, limbic resonance—that condition in which two people's physiological states become attuned—may be, well, more resonant, because the lovers' systems are more alike than those of a heterosexual pair.

There's an old joke in the gay community: what does a lesbian bring on the second date? A U-Haul. What does a gay guy bring? A friend.

There's some neurochemical truth to this joke. When two women have sex, the oxytocin surge can induce cuddling that lasts for days. Two male lovers, under the heavier influence of vasopressin, to say nothing of testosterone, may quickly feel ready to move on physically and emotionally after lovemaking.

In addition to the match in brain chemistry in same-sex couples, there's evidence that one partner—gay or straight—can absorb the other's sex and bonding chemicals; in a same-sex couple, this could heap on an extra helping of estrogen or testosterone. Estrogen and testosterone may be exchanged via lovers' sweat and saliva, according to preliminary research by Cameron Muir of Brock University (Holland 2006).

How do one person's sex steroids get into the other person's brain? Most mammals have a special area in the nose called the vomeronasal organ. This sensitive tissue, located in the nasal passages, sends molecules inhaled by the animal directly to the brain, where they can influence behavior. This organ reacts to pheromones, the chemical-signaling substances put out by many animals, from insects to apes. It's the organ that draws a female elephant to the musth secreted by a bull in his prime.

Human fetuses have a vomeronasal organ, and for a long time, biologists thought that it was a vestigial structure that disappeared by birth. But recently, researchers have found evidence that the human response to pheromones is alive and well in adults (Smith and Bhatnagar 2000). The vomeronasal organ seems to be responsible, for example, for the tendency of women living together to synchronize their menstrual cycles. It's possible that when you're very close to someone else—kissing or nuzzling, for example—you inhale minute amounts of his or her unique chemical perfume. This perfume could include oxytocin, which has been shown to increase feelings of trust when it's inhaled (Zak, Kurzban, and Matzner 2005).

These studies certainly don't prove anything about neural differences in gays and straights, but they make it clear that people of all sexual flavors do react to the neurochemicals they swap when they canoodle. This effect in a gay couple may reinforce their neurochemical states. Remember, estrogen increases the effects of oxytocin, while testosterone decreases them. So, with every nuzzle, taste, and touch, a same-sex pair creates a neurochemical feedback loop that reinforces the tendencies of their sex.

When two women engage in intimate behavior, from hanging out with a friend to wild lovemaking, it's likely that, with every breath, each takes in molecules of estrogen and oxytocin emitted by the other's body. Two men enjoying the same behaviors likely inhale each other's testosterone, oxytocin, and vasopressin. Overall, two women may experience more oxytocin in their relationship than a man and a woman, and two men may experience less oxytocin and more vasopressin and testosterone.

It's crucial to note here that the wide range of temperaments and tendencies in men and women certainly extends to gays and lesbians. Men, gay and straight, may find it extremely easy to bond, while women of all sexual persuasions run the gamut from runaround to stay-at-home. The important thing is that for all of us, gay and straight, the neurochemistry of bonding is the same.

Chapter 6

raising kids who trust and love

If we have to learn to love when we're babies, then parents clearly play a vital role in helping their children develop a healthy oxytocin response. While the first three years of life are the most important in forging the pathways of the brain's oxytocin system, the human brain continues to grow until the early twenties; so your work on helping to shape your child's brain goes on. Mothers and fathers can guide the next generation in growing up to become men and women who can accept the closeness they crave.

Recreating the Way We're Parented

We can read all the parenting books out there, but most of the way we parent comes from the way we were parented—unless we consciously learn new patterns. Moms, dads, and others who take care of babies can inadvertently transfer the negative responses they themselves learned, continuing a cycle of failed attachment that's passed down through the generations.

A study of 288 Texan couples expecting their first child looked at how their attachment styles influenced their feelings toward their babies (Wilson et al. 2007). Just two weeks after the babies were born, mothers with the avoidant attachment style—the ones who try to keep from being hurt by avoiding intimacy—didn't feel as close to their newborn babies as the other mothers did. Highly anxious women felt greater jealousy toward their babies than the other moms. Anxious fathers got in on the negativity too: they felt more jealous of their newborn competitors for Mom's attention.

Babies pick up on this quickly, and by the time they toddle, they've already learned their lesson. When the little boy expresses his normal needs, it triggers the mother's old insecurity or pain, preventing her from giving him what he needs. The child sees that needing his mom makes her feel bad, so he learns to hide his need. He's in a tragic situation: not only can he not get the nurturing he pines for from his mom, but he can't even express his yearning genuinely. He begins to develop the same insecurity and pain she feels, and he reflects this in the way he meets the world.

At the same time, he doesn't develop the oxytocin response that comes when you experience peace and safety as you're fed, as you look at your mother, and as she looks back at you with love.

Mean Like Mommy

A couple of experiments by Dario Maestripieri, a University of Chicago biologist, offer insight into how early mothering affects our brain's chemical responses later in life—as well as how we develop the urge to mother.

Since the 1990s, Maestripieri has worked with rhesus macaque monkeys. Socially, these monkeys aren't so much like humans. They're nonmonogamous; females live in matrilineal groups, sharing food and casually lending a hand with each other's babies. Males hang out with each other, fighting for dominance; they occasionally stop by the females to copulate or steal food. But if you want to look at the attachment between mother and baby, they're a perfect model: rhesus females have one baby at a time, and they invest years in its care, just as humans do.

Observing the rhesus colony at the Yerkes Primate Center in Atlanta, Maestripieri noticed that the rhesus monkeys' mothering styles were as varied as humans'. Even before they became mothers, some females just loved to touch and hold babies, but some were about as maternal as Joan Crawford. When they had babies of their own, some of them doted, and some were downright abusive. So, Maestripieri began a systematic look at how the rhesus monkeys' hormones changed with time and experience (Maestripieri 2003). He compared the mothers' estrogen, progesterone, and prolactin levels and tracked them over time but found no differences. He tried manipulating their endogenous opioids, the beta-endorphins that get us naturally high—nothing.

Next, he looked at the role of early experiences. Right after birth, he switched around some newborn monkeys, giving the babies of good mothers to bad mothers, and letting the good mothers raise the babies of abusive females. The children of aggressive mothers tended to be aggressive themselves—even though they were raised by sweet mothers. The same held true for sociability; the babies of irritable, unfriendly mothers tended to react to others the same way, even though they grew up in a cordial clan. This showed that an individual's tendency to be sweet or mean may be inherited.

But when Maestripieri looked at the brain chemicals of baby monkeys, he found that the kind of mothering they got did matter—a lot (2005). Some of the babies who were regularly rejected by their mothers—being pushed away when they tried to climb into her arms, for example—had up to 20 percent less serotonin, a neurotransmitter that's a mood elevator. Low levels of serotonin are associated with depression, anxiety, and impulsive aggression in monkeys and humans. The more rejection a baby experienced, the less serotonin it produced, and these low levels continued into adulthood. Some of these low-serotonin monkeys themselves went on to become bad mothers.

While serotonin isn't a direct part of the oxytocin-attachment system, the two brain chemicals are closely related. Serotonin stimulates the release of both oxytocin and vasopressin (Jorgensen et al. 2003). Therefore, it's a good bet that monkeys and humans with low levels of serotonin don't experience as strong of an oxytocin response. They may not bond as deeply; they may not be able to bond at all.

111

About half of the abused monkey babies, however, went on to become relatively good mothers. And they didn't have lowered serotonin levels. It's possible that they inherited more resilience to stress and more oxytocin-rich parasympathetic nervous systems from their loving mamas. This is reassuring to all of us who didn't get the kind of mothering we wish we had. We can overcome both "nature" and "nurture" to raise children who are even more secure and more loving than we are.

heal thyself

Even if you feel you missed out on forming the deepest attachment with your baby, you can learn to strengthen the bond and deepen your oxytocin response as your child grows. Take advantage of neural plasticity—the potential for growth and change that's inherent in your brain cells—to open yourself to deeper love. Working on your relationship with your child can be a very powerful force for change.

Bryan Post is a therapist who has gained recognition for his ability to heal extremely troubled kids with an approach that takes into account the dynamics of the whole family. Post himself was an adopted and disruptive child. Now, at the Post Institute for Family-Centered Therapy in Oklahoma City and in workshops around the country, he helps parents learn to provide the brain-shaping experiences their children missed.

Post thinks that a parent's own attachment issues can get in the way of seeing that a child's out-of-control behavior comes from fear, not maliciousness, defiance, or an evil nature, as it often seems (Post 2007). Once parents can remove their own fears from the relationship, it's easier for them to heal the child's fear. Sessions with parents begin with whatever behaviors or problems seem most critical to them. While the end goal certainly is to help the child develop into a loving, happy, and responsible member of the family, these first steps are as much about guiding the parents into a deeper understanding of themselves.

For example, some kids lie, often gleefully and gratuitously. Post coaches parents to ignore this for a while. But a father might protest that it's something he just can't ignore. Well, why not? It may be that his own father lied to him. If this father can understand that his anger at his son comes from this old wound, he can begin to stop projecting his anger onto his son's behavior.

Says Post, "When they understand who they are in relationship to the child, and become more mindful of their own fear, it helps them to understand the child at a deeper level" (Post 2007). Parents come to the Post Institute to help their children, but in the process they also heal themselves. Your relationship with your child provides a potent opportunity to grow together. Your own heart will open as your child blossoms.

Fathering

We've examined mothering, defined as the central relationship between a baby and the person who takes care of him the most. We've seen how a newborn learns to generalize the oxytocin response from the primary caregiver to other people in the family, and then to an ever-widening circle of relationships. And we've examined how the differences in men's and women's chemical makeup—especially differences in the sex hormones—may flavor their moods and behavior.

While women do seem to be the world's primary child tenders, men, too, have evolved to help out—and not only by fending off bears and wolves. Even though male hormones damp down the mechanisms by which oxytocin makes the hand want to rock the cradle, men do, in fact, rock the cradle—as well as sometimes build the cradle. Still, men may "mother" differently. In fact, there's a word for the way men mother: we call it fathering. We defined "mother" as the person who is the primary caregiver; let's define "father" as a child's primary male relationship. (While a man may mother, in this case we're looking specifically at a male-flavored kind of care.)

When a man becomes a father, it's more than a change in lifestyle. The experience actually remodels his brain and neurochemistry just as much as pregnancy does a woman's. Vasopressin readies him to respond to challenge by amping up his sympathetic nervous system. In a challenge, vasopressin overrules the effect of oxytocin, turning off trust and friendly behavior. You'll recall that testosterone increases his energy and self-confidence, making him more willing to be aggressive.

That twist that vasopressin gives to the male brain goes a long way toward explaining how differences between mothering and fathering might have come to be. As previously mentioned, in primitive times, a woman's best chance to keep her children safe from danger was to hide, and oxytocin calmed her enough to do that. But fighting to protect his family was a man's best strategy for passing along his genes.

The male may be the more expendable of the pair, but the experience of manliness is not expendable. We evolved in a world of men and women, and children should experience both flavors of humanity. Girls and boys need loving role models of both sexes to help them learn to understand and be comfortable with this essential difference.

Mothering and Fathering, for Boys and Girls

Touch remains the foundation for healthy emotional growth as children learn to walk and then run. Without a steady diet of safe physical intimacy, children may grow up with "skin hunger," a craving to be touched and held in a way that involves the whole body, not just the socially sanctioned safe areas of face and hands (Mainous 2002).

Unfortunately, touching even our own children is becoming increasingly problematic in our society. An appropriate awareness of the problem of sexual abuse combined with cultural norms make it especially difficult for some fathers to feel that they can freely offer physical affection. The rules of macho keep some men from reaching out—literally—except with their lovers and spouses. Because of this idea of manliness, in a lot of families, touch deprivation begins early for boy children. Bruises and hurts are soothed with a quick pat; rough-and-tumble play takes the place of cuddling so that the kid won't grow up to be a sissy. Homophobia means boys must never touch their friends. Girls, too, may suffer from the lack of loving, nonsexual touch from the men in their families, especially as they grow out of the toddler stage.

As your children grow up, your mothering and fathering styles may change to accommodate their need to differentiate from you while maintaining healthy touch.

114

Raging Hormones

As they approach puberty, and the sex hormones simmer in their veins, children need as much attention and physical contact as ever, even though they've reached a stage where they're more interested in their peers than their families. Skin-hungry kids may turn to sex play just because it feels wonderful to be held. An adolescent who gets plenty of hugs and strokes at home, on the other hand, will be able to keep a clearer head on dates.

Maintaining your kids' oxytocin advantage as they move into adolescence requires understanding how puberty affects the brain and the oxytocin systems of boys and girls. Our divergent endocrine systems have evolved in ways that helped each sex survive and thrive in prehistoric times, according to David Geary and Mark Flinn, of the University of Missouri (2002). Men needed to form alliances outside the immediate family, and the more allies they had, the more powerful they would be. Therefore, evolution favored weaker bonds that were easily formed and weren't as high-maintenance as women's friendships.

According to Geary and Flinn's theory, males show an "evolved fight response"; that is, over time they've learned to harness aggressive impulses in socially beneficial ways. For example, games, bragging, and rough-housing among groups of male friends are ways of acting out aggression, but at the same time, they strengthen the affection between them and solidify the group.

Women, on the other hand, were more likely to survive a threat, and thereby ensure that the children survived, if they stayed quiet with the children in a safe place, according to UCLA psychologist Shelley Taylor (Taylor et al. 2000). Taylor's "tend and befriend" theory maintains that friendships with other women were a different way to ensure that a woman passed on her genes. A woman who was good at forming alliances would get more help and support at all times; if she were injured or killed, one of her friends might be willing to adopt her offspring.

As adolescent boys and girls flirt and date, you could say they're practicing for the time when they'll pair up in marriage, whether or not they play the gender roles that developed in ancient times. But adolescence is where boys and girls first encounter the trick that nature has played on the human race. As we head toward sexual maturity, the sex hormones exert a profound influence on oxytocin, driving a chasm between the attachment systems of boys and girls. In the desire-ridden adolescent body, lust is spiked by testosterone, one of the steroids that creates weird new feelings, strange thoughts, and profound changes in the body and brain of both males and females. But estrogen's amplifying effect on oxytocin gives a girl's lust a very different flavor.

Girls: Touch-Sensitive in an Oversexed World

Estrogen and oxytocin go together like chocolate and milk. In the female brain, estrogen increases the amount of oxytocin taken up by receptors, while progesterone emphasizes its effects (Bale et al. 2001; Schumacher et al. 1990). Estrogen causes some of the genes in the hypothalamus to express themselves by creating more oxytocin receptors (Witt, Carter, and Insel 1991). The massive jolts of estrogen to a girl's system that begin when she hits puberty increase oxytocin production as they sprinkle additional oxytocin receptors throughout her social brain. At the same time, estrogen scatters more oxytocin receptors throughout the uterus and mammary glands. Those receptors will be needed if she becomes pregnant, when they'll respond to signals from the brain and the developing fetus that will eventually cause her uterus to contract and milk to flow from her breasts (Insel 1997).

This confluence of estrogen and oxytocin gives teenage girls an irresistible desire to bond—with anyone and anything (Brizendine 2006). Oxytocin release, along with rewarding gushes of dopamine, is triggered by all the social minutiae of middle school, and these gratifying hormonal spurts can seem like the most important things in the world. That's why girls can become as deeply attached to pets and celebrities as to the people around them, as they seek a constant supply of these feel-good "drugs" (Odendaal and Meintjes 2003).

boy trouble

And then, there are boys. If a girl ditches her friends, lets her grades slip, and drops out of soccer to play the dating game, it's because her brain's motivation circuits are entirely taken up by the pursuit of romance. Her breast may tingle if a boy accidentally—or on purpose—brushes against it. But that same touch can strike up her all-too-willing bonding process. Her sexual desire may be more inchoate but no less intense than a boy's. She may not even connect the flushes that run across her skin and make her squirm in her classroom seat to sex.

No matter how well connected she is to her family, after puberty, she forms the most intense bond of all with the boy or boys who touch her—at a time when the effects of oxytocin in those boys are at their lowest. This hormonal mismatch pits girls against boys in a competition to get their needs met. Boys crave connection, too, according to psychotherapist and author Michael Gurian (1996). But they express it through aggressive physical action—and it's natural to extend that to girls. The boy-girl wrestling matches in cars, on picnic blankets, and in parents' basements is part of the basic male bonding strategy and is perhaps not so different from the playful wrestling boys do with their male friends.

Except, of course, they aren't trying to pin their friends down so they can feel their genitals—and impregnate them in the bargain. Girls have to take into account that a boy's drive for sex in these circumstances is stronger than his drive for emotional intimacy. Boys quickly learn to use the language of romance to get girls, but for many of them, it's a foreign tongue they'll never feel comfortable with. When a boy tells a girl he loves her, especially after sex, he may mean it. After all, he's experienced the same oxytocin rush at orgasm that she has. But, while the high tide of estrogen prolongs that rush in her system, his subsides in a matter of minutes.

During this period in her life, changes in the family may deprive a girl of the source of love, support, and oxytocin she has relied on: her parents. This is the life stage when a couple that's stayed together for the kids' sake divorces, the time when stay-at-home mothers return to work. The family may be all too happy to heed the girl's demands to "just leave me alone!" (Gurian 2007).

So her friends become fountains of oxytocin and dopamine, as chatting, giggling, dishing dirt, and sharing secrets fire the neurons in their brains' trust and attachment circuits. However, while these girls' social and emotional brains are running at full speed, their cerebral cortexes, designed to run the show and make decisions that will benefit the organism as a whole, haven't fully matured. Girls' cliques and peer groups don't always have the collective wisdom needed to navigate the dangerous waters of a modern adolescence.

too sexy?

As she nears puberty, a girl's play focuses more and more on mate seeking. She may still enjoy babysitting or taking care of pets, but a pubescent girl's motivation system narrows the goal to being desirable. Desire, however, may come before she's physically or emotionally ready for it. The age of puberty has plummeted in the last 165 years, rushing girls into a sexual maturity that their brains and emotions can't keep up with (Bellis, Downing, and Ashton 2006). In 1840, girls in France, the nation with the earliest available statistics, didn't start menstruating until they were nearly fifteen. In the United States in 1860, the first year this was tracked, the average age was over sixteen.

By 1960, the average onset of menarche was between thirteen and thirteen-and-a-half in France, and twelve-and-a-half in the United States. Today, most girls in developed nations reach puberty in their twelfth year (Bellis, Downing, and Ashton 2006; Herman-Giddens et al. 1997). While much of this change reflects better nutrition and health, another cause of accelerated puberty is stress, according to research from the John Moores University Centre for Public Health in the United Kingdom (Bellis, Downing, and Ashton 2006). Divorced parents and absentee fathers are two of the stressors the researchers identified as puberty pushers. This points out the strong role for fathering—from all the men who are close to a girl, as well as her biological father—for a girl's physical development and the development of her brain.

Another culprit is body fat: *leptin*, a protein made by fat cells, controls appetite and the packing on of body fat, and it also helps trigger puberty (Kaplowitz 2004). As supersizing kids get plumper and plumper, their sexual development may come faster and faster.

But there's a huge gap between physical puberty, the physical ability and drive to have sex, and social puberty, the development of the neo-cortical integration of thought and emotion that allows a girl to make intelligent choices about sex.

Think about the differences between a sixteen-year-old girl and a twelve-year-old. The teenager has grown close to her full height, and has fully formed breasts and a full growth of pubic and underarm hair. This hair growth is caused not by estrogen but by androgens, including testosterone, and it signals the development of sexual desire. The sixteen-year-old's body is ready to procreate, and her brain is mature enough to control at least some of her impulses.

The twelve-year-old is still a child, physically and mentally. Any adult can see that she's not ready for sex. Girls who experience premature puberty tend to have their first boyfriends a year earlier than normal, and have sex twenty-one months earlier than girls who go through puberty at the normal age (Kaplowitz 2004). Sex education in the United States starts—if it starts at all—in fifth grade, and while it explains the mechanics of procreation, it seldom goes beyond advising kids to say no at a time when every cell in their bodies says yes. The media and merchandising industries are right on top of this trend, say the London researchers: there are lines of makeup and perfume for the preteen set, and clothes that wouldn't look out of place on a hooker. But the social structures that could help girls deal with their new bodies haven't kept up. This lack of support can have lifelong consequences.

When girls are left to figure out for themselves that the love they get from boys isn't the same as the love they give, the trouble they find can color their whole lives. The best protection against this fate is making sure daughters receive loving physical contact as well as emotional support. If their thirst for connection can be slaked by many different people, they're more likely to have the resources to help them make wise decisions about sex and romance.

Sex education should include education about the neurochemistry of sex. Girls should learn that bonding is a likely effect of physical intimacy—not necessarily a response to the other person. The feeling is, "He's the only one for me." But the reality is, "Because we touched, I now *feel as if* he's the only one for me." This reframing of the feeling can put it in perspective—and may encourage girls to think more carefully about whether they want to become bonded with a particular boy.

Boys: Testosterone Time Bombs

As their bodies mature, boys may struggle with reconciling their own needs for connection with a new set of impulses for sex, competition, and physical activity. When he reaches puberty, a boy begins to experience surges of *DHT*, a more potent kind of testosterone than that which has been circulating in his body. Five to seven times a day, this hormone will flood his body, increasing his overall testosterone levels to ten or even fifty times a girl's (Gurian 1996). Boys' war games also raise their levels of testosterone and cortisol, making them, well, more like boys—and even more alien to girls. Our sex-and-violence-drenched media environment stokes the fires. A steady diet of TV mayhem may cause an earlier and stronger release of testosterone in a boy, pushing him into an early puberty that his brain and emotions aren't prepared to handle (Bernhardt et al. 1998).

the testosterone fire

With puberty, his penis grows as much as eight times bigger, and it becomes a strange bedfellow, turning the nights into sweaty, half-waking dreams of desire. By day, it leaps into action at inappropriate and embarrassing times, turning the most innocent interactions into secret erotic interludes. Now begins the famous (although not scientifically documented) obsession: sexual thoughts every two minutes.

As his muscles thicken and his skin sprouts hair, a boy's brain changes as well. His brain began to differentiate from a female's *in utero*, when his X-Y chromosome combo stimulated surges of testosterone that caused some areas of the brain to grow faster and forge neural pathways that differ from a female's brain.

This new torrent of testosterone will extend and reinforce those differences in his brain, while a new round of neural pruning will pare down his synapses: if he hasn't used a system of neurons, he'll lose it. He'll tend to be better at spatial relationships than emotional ones. He may have a fine memory for statistics and facts, while seeing no need to distinguish between the colors peach and beige (Verrelli and Tishkoff 2004). His *corpus callosum*, the band of fibers connecting the two hemispheres of the brain, won't grow as fast or as large as a girl's, making it less likely that he'll be able to integrate different processes, such as language and emotion. His amygdala, the seat of emotional reactions, will grow larger. And, when he senses danger, his fight-or-flight reflexes will kick in quicker than a girl's, making him more likely to act before he thinks (Rubinow, Schmidt, and Roca 2002).

defining the male brain

His brain will tend to idle in reptilian mode, where responses lash out automatically. He may also feel social pressure to be more assertive, less reflective, and less empathetic. These two forces make him apt to react to stress with aggression or destruction. His reactions make it less attractive for others to comfort him, thereby further upping his stress level. At this point in the growth of his brain, the emotion-integrating, decision-making prefrontal cortex hasn't kept up with the brawny amygdala, so there's no hand on the throttle. Aggression, rage, and sex are the wild cards that turn male puberty into a game of high-stakes risk.

His male hormones drive him to crave thrills and even danger. He loves to compete. He's more ready to fight when he's angry, and also when he's depressed or frightened. Because his prefrontal cortex isn't as well developed as his amygdala, he becomes more prone than girls to suffer from conduct disorders and more likely to abuse drugs and alcohol (Kessler et. al 2005).

evolutionary imperative to sex and violence

And he wants sex—as much of it as he can get, with as many partners as possible. This evolutionary leftover impels him to spread his seed as widely as possible, to maximize his reproductive potential. This puts boys in a hormonal dilemma. We are a monogamous species, biologically primed to live with one mate and cooperate in raising children—even if we occasionally copulate with others.

Females fit right into this scenario, as estrogen fluffs the oxytocin impulse to bond and nest. But boys are torn: testosterone increases their brains' receptivity to vasopressin, a hormone of vigilance and aggression, as it mutes the soothing effects of oxytocin. Mommy's love, the security of cuddling, and the peace of being rocked are faint memories in the androgens' red glare. The flood of testosterone ensures that almost any touching with girls will be highly sexual, and without a well-developed oxytocin response, there may be none of the bonding that should also accompany touch. No wonder modern men are so angry. No wonder there are so many single mothers with children who never see their daddies.

Here's where nurturing can play a role in the development of a boy's personality: males *do* respond to the calming, bonding effects of oxytocin, and being with someone supportive increases these effects—even when support comes from another male (Heinrichs et al. 2003). That support may not look so touchy-feely, but it's real. Allies—the guys who "have his back"—cool out his fiery impulses, while the nonstop jostling and insults guys trade are a rough form of love (Gurian 2007). Even if a boy has a good attachment to his mother, at puberty he needs a strong bond with an older male who can initiate him into a style of manhood that includes inhibiting his impulses and finding healthy outlets for his aggression.

finding a hero

Michael Gurian has devoted his career to helping parents raise "good sons" to be "good men." He encourages boys to think of their lives as the same kind of hero quest that inspires the movies and books they love. He says, "If not before, then at least by the time he's about sixteen, a boy needs to become clear on the fundamental principles of his own life quest. If he does not do this, he will wander unhappily for many decades through an unforgiving society. ... To be a man, you have to live your life as a mission" (Gurian 1999, 36).

This exhortation brilliantly exploits boys' natural hormonal instincts and turns them toward socially adaptive ends. When a boy defines his life as a quest for meaning, he invokes vasopressin's help in turning his urges toward what Gurian calls "compassionate action" (Gurian 1999, 721). Instead of being a hapless bundle of aggression, he becomes a crusader who'll fight, when necessary, against obstacles in his path.

Families Take Charge

It's up to parents to help their boys manage this transition from child-hood to adulthood. Gurian (1998) believes that in adolescence boys need intense training along with their secure base of love within the family. Adults should provide challenges and adventures that answer testosterone's and vasopressin's push for aggression. You can see how computer games provide exactly the progressive challenge, reward, and access to secret knowledge that also takes place in tribal initiations. As a gamer gains skills, he's rewarded with more power and talismans he can use to compete with others, whether real or virtual. He slays mon-sters, travels through unknown lands, and sees marvels. The problem with games is that, when the game is over, the boy is alone in his room. He may form bonds with others over the Internet—and there's evidence that interacting over the computer can provoke an oxytocin response (Zak et al. 2005). But these virtual friends are not available to share the perils and joys of daily life the way a friend who lived nearby would be.

Gurian believes that, because boys often don't connect quickly with others by talking about their feelings, they need more opportunities for connection than girls do, and with more people outside the family. In fact, he thinks we've let our boys and men down by insisting that they bond the way females do. He insists that it's men's job to raise the next generation of boys. The way to do this, he writes in *A Fine Young Man* (1998), is to provide plenty of different circumstances in which boys can find friendship.

Circumstances of friendship are the myriad events and situations in which we're brought into regular contact with others, allowing us to move from respect to trust to connection. Such circumstances include sports teams, clubs, spiritual or religious organizations, neighborhoods, and extended families. In our overachieving and highly mobile culture, kids may live far from their relatives, or be separated from mentors and friends when the family moves or parents divorce. While such ruptures of the social fabric may be inevitable, parents can nevertheless recog-nize their boys' need for these opportunities and provide plenty of new circumstances in which they can find mentors.

It also means accepting "male nurturance systems" that may not seem to mesh with the values and interests of the parents. For example, school sports are an established way of harnessing boys' energy and competitive drives, while bonding them together as a team, with their coach as the leader. But some parents fear that going out for a school team opens a boy to the possibility of humiliation, injury, or a hyperaggressive "jock" culture. Churches, temples, or mosques are organized to teach values and idealism while providing a supportive community, yet less than half of Americans attend church regularly, according to a 2007 Gallup poll (Newport 2007).

When you understand your boy's need for relationships that let him form oxytocin bonds while answering the drive of testosterone and vasopressin for competition and challenge, you can find circumstances of friendship that fit with your own beliefs and inclinations. For example, if you don't want your son to become a jock, explore martial arts practices, such as capoeira or aikido, which focus on strength, determination, and self-control under the guidance of an authoritative teacher. Learning to use guns and hunting is a male rite of passage that harks back to our ancient ways. If this is abhorrent to you, volunteer with your son to work on wildlife habitat restoration projects in your community. The hard work will give him a sense of accomplishment and mastery—in a good way—over nature.

The Oxytocin Advantage

Raising children who trust and love is important not only for their interpersonal relationships; these abilities also stand them in good stead in every aspect of life, giving them advantages that extend to school and the workplace. By the age of seven, secure children begin to outperform their less well-attached peers when it comes to grades (Jacobsen and Hofmann 1997). Adolescents with supportive parents and friends think and concentrate better. They do better in school, getting higher grades on tests in high school and college. These kids also have more positive attitudes about work and feel more confident about their ability to choose a career.

The differences may show up in high school, but they really manifest themselves when teenagers leave home to go to college (Larose,

Bernier, and Tarabulsy 2005). Secure adolescents can devote more of their emotional resources to succeeding in college, while the normal stress of a new and challenging environment may activate the inefficient coping strategies of avoidant and anxiously attached teenagers, making the transition that much harder.

When Simon Larose and colleagues of Laval University in Quebec looked at how well sixty-two freshmen adapted to the demands of their new academic environment, they found that secure students maintained their good study habits or even improved them (Larose, Bernier, and Tarabulsy 2005). On the other hand, the insecurely attached students had more trouble with their studies than they had in high school. The anxious students were more afraid of failing, and felt less comfortable asking teachers for help. Nevertheless, they gave less priority to their studies than the secure students. A related study found that their grade-point averages dropped from the high-school averages (Bernier et al. 2004).

The harm of these dysfunctional behaviors blights far more than a student's transcript. The inability to connect in the academic world puts a damper on forging the kinds of relationships that can help adults succeed in their careers. An academic mentor steers her protégées toward crucial course work and advises them on where they should focus their energies. She makes sure they get the best internships, meet the most important people, and get appointments with the most desirable recruiters. A phone call from her to an old colleague can put a graduating student's résumé on the top of the pile; a glowing letter of recommendation can secure a place in the best graduate program. But students who expect to be rejected by their professors or are too frightened to approach them will never spark the interest and affection that inspires an older person to guide them.

Naturally, these poor work habits don't magically disappear the day these students graduate from college. Just as the stress of transitioning from high school to college seemed to activate some adolescents' dysfunctional coping strategies, the greater stress of having to function as an adult in the workplace may knock them down another notch.

Loving Generations

Both women and men have a role to play in making sure the children they care for learn to form healthy and appropriate oxytocin responses. As that child goes out into the world, he or she will encounter societal pressures that may be at odds with the need for safe intimacy. And, as every boy and girl reaches puberty, each will experience nature's pressure to procreate in the form of potentially overwhelming sexual desire. No matter what the configuration of the family in which a child grows, it's likely that boys will look to men as potential models for at least some aspects of themselves, as girls look to women. In our sexually obsessed and intimacy-challenged culture, you can guide your children to a more nuanced and rounded humanity—one that's open to trust and generosity, one that embraces closeness.

Parenting children who maintain strong oxytocin bonds as they grow through the stages into adulthood means finding ways to maintain physical and emotional intimacy with you as they begin to look outside the family for the neurochemical rewards of connection. You may need to get very creative to lure them into circumstances of friendship—and endure plenty of frustration when they approach puberty and act as if they hate you. When you understand and support your child's unique expression of the interaction between biology, culture, and your family's flavor, you'll rise to the challenge of producing an adult with the ability to give and get the love we all need.

The Cow-Tipping Game

When children reach school age, they're often less willing to cuddle; the moments when they sit on your lap gazing into your eyes may be rare. There are plenty of other ways to enjoy warm physical contact in the family. This exercise was developed by relationship counselors Reid Mihalko and Marcia Baczynski, who kindly provided their permission to publish it here. It's a fun thing to do in your family, and because there's an element of rough-and-tumble, it will appeal to the less cuddly members.

1. Use a carpeted, comfortable room. Clear a space big enough for everyone to sit on the floor. Take off your shoes.

2. Get on your hands and knees—all of you. Pretend you're contented cows in a beautiful green field. You can mill around, facing each other or hanging out side by side.

3. Begin nudging and leaning into each other. Draw closer and lean harder, until you topple into a heap.

4. You can stay sprawled in the heap, get up and do it again, or dust yourself off and go about your day.

Chapter 7

feathering the nest

because oxytocin is at the root of every kind of positive social interaction, opportunities to enjoy its healing, happy effects can be woven throughout your day. Every person you meet is an opportunity to renew or strengthen your oxytocin response—or to begin to build it. Every day is a new chance to learn to connect.

It's Never Too Late

We sometimes feel anger or deep yearning about not having gotten the kind of love we needed to thrive when we were children. It's easy to look back at our lives and grieve over missed opportunities for growth and connection. But it's not too late. Don't forget about neural plasticity: the way our brains continue to grow and change throughout our lives. Science is only beginning to understand the regenerative powers of the brain. People with massive brain damage from stroke have learned to walk and talk again. The brains of people whose inner ears are damaged rewire themselves to make sense of the electronic signals from cochlear implants. In fact, the basic concept of neural plasticity is that exercising groups of neurons makes them work faster and more efficiently (Doidge 2007). Clearly, neural plasticity supports the brain's ability to change, learn, and grow throughout our lives.

Therefore, it makes sense that you can strengthen your oxytocin response the same way you'd strengthen a weak muscle in your shoulder. Unless you're a fire spotter or you're sailing solo around the world, your days are filled with human interactions of all kinds. Every one of these interactions gives you a chance to learn or practice the oxytocin response.

We'll move from solo techniques through group activities to one-on-one connections, as we look at everyday activities that strengthen our "connection muscles." It's important to dip in at the point where you feel comfortable. If you learned as a child that intimacy was dangerous or hurtful, you might want to start your practice with yourself. You can also combine individual and group activities. And you don't have to try these activities step by step; do whatever attracts you, and combine activities for alone time and together time.

Here's one caveat: the idea that the more oxytocin you produce, the better you feel is a gross oversimplification. Sometimes, chronically stressed people and animals have higher levels of oxytocin in their blood. It's possible that this is the body's attempt to cool down the stress response, but it's also possible that the elevated hormone level is a sign that the brain, in its harried state, can't use oxytocin effectively (Carter 2007b). This state could be analogous to a diabetic's high blood sugar. Oxytocin, like glucose, may not be able to get into the cells to do its good work. So, the idea of "getting more oxytocin" remains scientifically groundless. But, if you think of boosting oxytocin in the context of activating the parasympathetic nervous system to induce the three Rs of rest, relaxation, and repair, you won't go wrong with these techniques.

Things to Do by Yourself

Sometimes it doesn't feel natural or good to reach out to others; sometimes we're in situations where we need to go it alone for a while. And sometimes, frankly, the idea of opening up to someone else is just too scary. Just as you wouldn't begin a physical exercise program by trying to run a marathon, you should start exercising your oxytocin response in simple, private ways.

Your Calm and Connection Spot

When stress goes up, so does cortisol. On the other hand, oxytocin's role in the birth process seems to be facilitated by a quiet, safe-seeming environment. So it makes sense that creating a soothing retreat for yourself can be an excellent first step toward increasing the oxytocin opportunities in your life.

While few of us have the kind of home seen in magazines, all of us can find one spot we can designate as the chill zone, the home base within the home. Your calm and connection spot can be as small as a corner with a chair and lamp, or a hammock on the porch. If you live with others, it's a bit delicate to balance sharing the home space with your need for a personal chill spot, but the important thing is that *you* design the spot, whether or not other people use it too.

Just as sleep experts advise you not to do anything but sleep and make love in your bed, you should only go to your calm and connection spot when you either feel relaxed and calm or need to cool down. Over time, you may find that your parasympathetic nervous system automatically kicks in when you arrive at your spot.

design for you

Your personal home base begins with at least one place to sit or recline; it should be very comfortable. The colors in this area should be ones you enjoy. If you don't have a strong color preference, apply the rules of color theory. Blue is considered a calming color, while green evokes healing, tranquility, and rebirth. On the warm side, shades of orange seem friendly and comforting, while yellow cheers (Sawahata and Eldridge 2007). Select artwork, photographs, plants, an aquarium—things that attract your eye as you sit. Please your other senses as well. A seat by a window will let you cast your eyes into the distance, and contemplate colors and textures outside your room. Include a variety of lighting options, such as a candle, a small lamp with a colored bulb, a reading lamp, and an overhead light fixture with a dimmer.

Don't forget to please your ears. If you like to listen to music, add a music player stocked with tunes that lead you into a quiet state; this is not the place to listen to show tunes, hip-hop, rock, or marching bands. If you live in a noisy environment, consider a white-noise generator. These machines put out sounds that cancel out background noise while remaining in the back of your consciousness. A tabletop fountain is another option for disguising background noise, providing distraction for your eyes and ears.

If this all seems tedious or a waste of time, remind yourself that oxytocin promotes caring behavior, and caring behavior promotes oxytocin. Taking the time to select furnishings and accoutrements that please you is a form of self-care, an affirmation that your needs are important. Remember that "comfort" means both a state of well-being and the act of offering solace.

practice peace

Don't wait to enjoy your personal zone of tranquility until everything is just so. Once you have the basics of a comfortable seat and pleasant lighting, you can begin to practice self-soothing, and then add objects and decor as you like. For example, if your eyes continually come to rest on a tabletop, you can place a beautiful item there.

At first, it may seem hard to settle down and rest, but over time, this spot will act as a cue for your body to move into a calmer state. You can help this process along by using relaxation techniques. If you've already found methods that work for you, such as meditation, self-hypnosis, or visualization, you can now indulge in these in your special spot. You can also try this simple practice adapted from *The Daily Relaxer*, by Matthew McKay and Patrick Fanning (2006).

Quick-Release Relaxer

This exercise helps you to consciously release tension in one part of your body at a time. At the same time, it lets you turn your calm spot into a cue that encourages your body to relax automatically whenever you sit there. As you do this exercise, pay attention to changes in each muscle group.

1. Sit or lie comfortably. Take a deep breath and hold it as you mentally count to seven. Notice how the air expands your chest and belly. Release the breath slowly, counting backward from seven to one.

2. As you take another deep breath, make fists with both hands and tighten your forearms, biceps, and pectoral muscles. Clench as hard as you can as you count to seven, and then release the tension. Does your chest feel more open? Do your arms seem lighter?

3. Wrinkle every muscle of your face and neck. Squint, frown, pinch your lips, and hunch your shoulders for seven seconds. Then, let it all go. Again, look for differences in how those muscle groups feel.

4. Gently arch your back and inhale deeply into your chest. Hold your breath as you maintain this position for as long as is comfortable, and then relax as you exhale.

5. As you take another deep breath, push out your stomach as far as it will go. Try to make a huge Buddha belly. Hold for seven seconds, or as long as is comfortable, and then let your breath and belly go. Enjoy the quick whoosh of air as your stomach retracts.

6. Now, tighten all your stand-and-sit muscles: flex your feet and point your toes up and out. Clench your buttocks, thighs, and calves. Hold, and then relax.

7. Finally, point your toes as you again flex your buttocks, thighs, and calves to engage different muscles in your legs. Hold and then enjoy this final release.

8. Remain comfortably in place as you let your gaze idly travel around. If your eyes come to rest on an object, continue to look at it without staring or locking your eyes. Instead, move your eyes slowly across it, noticing every detail of its color, shape, and texture. When it feels right, continue to look around.

When you go to your personal home base, allow at least fifteen minutes to rest and enjoy it. Over time, you may not need to engage in any conscious practices in order for the oxytocin response to kick in. Once your body understands that when you come here, it's time to relax, you can also try inviting someone to share this time with you, with the understanding that this is an occasion to be quiet, not to chitchat. As you share this time with him or her, you may begin to feel a deeper connection.

Originally published in slightly different form in *The Daily Relaxer*, Matthew McKay and Patrick Fanning (Oakland, CA: New Harbinger Publications, 2006), 20–27. Adapted with permission of the authors and publisher.

Comfort Food

Let's face it, eating feels good. Nature made it rewarding so that, in the pre-civilization times when we were scroungers, we'd eat whenever we could. Food activates a number of the brain's reward areas, possibly including those areas in which oxytocin receptors tie social memory to reward in monogamous mammals (Beaver et al. 2006). There certainly seems to be a link between the pleasure of food and the pleasure of company. We may eat when we're lonely or when we feel rejected. Are food and social rewards handled by overlapping brain systems? Does oxytocin play a role in each? It certainly feels that way. There's evidence that eating and sex stimulate an oxytocin release that closely mimics that of being fed at the breast. Therefore, you can and should eat to comfort yourself—but in the right way.

why food equals love

There's a very direct connection between oxytocin and eating. Oxytocin helps moderate digestion, and it's directly related to satiety, that happy full-tummy feeling—which goes a long way toward explaining why we turn to food when we're lonely or sad (Evans 1997). The gut is dense with nerves, and it's at one end of the major pathway of the parasympathetic nervous system: the *vagus nerve* is a thick bundle of neurons running up and down the trunk of the body that's the major pathway for communication between the brain and both the digestive system and the genitals.

The gut is full of receptors for oxytocin and every other chemical found in the brain. It's also a major endocrine producer in its own right, pumping out the same chemicals that the brain uses to transmit messages, including serotonin and oxytocin (Pert 1997). John Furness (2006), a professor of cell biology at the University of Melbourne, points out that its interior is the largest surface exposed to the external world: with all its twists and convolutions and protrusions, its area is much greater than that of the skin. No wonder eating can be so satisfying.

Food in the stomach stimulates the secretion of gastric juices and digestive hormones, including insulin, leptin, and *cholecystokinin* (CCK). As they begin to digest the food, leptin and CCK also signal the brain via the vagus nerve. In response, the hypothalamus releases oxytocin, helping to produce that replete feeling. The satiety effect may be the result of oxytocin's sensitizing the brain to CCK's effects (Blevins 2008; Blevins et al. 2003; Blevins, Truong, and Gietzen 2004), as well as to oxytocin's causing the smooth muscles of the gut to contract (Uvnäs Moberg 2003). Now, here's a fascinating hint at the physiological link between food and love. In one of the early oxytocin experiments Kerstin Uvnäs Moberg participated in, she and her colleagues blocked the effect of CCK in newborn lambs. The result? The lambs lost their preference for their mothers (Nowak et al. 1997).

why food equals sex

Sex may be connected to eating, because it, too, signals the brain via the vagus nerve. Barry Komisaruk and Beverly Whipple of Rutgers

(2005) were the first to scan the brain during orgasm, when they used fMRI to observe the neural activity of women with spinal cord injuries as they masturbated. Researchers had assumed that, because spinal cord injuries cut off feeling to the lower part of the body, these women wouldn't be able to feel anything from sex either.

Wrong! The scientists found that these women could orgasm—and some of the women were thrilled to discover this, because they'd believed their doctors and had never tried masturbation or sex since their injuries.

If the connection between the spinal cord and brain had been severed, how did these women climax? The scientists found the alternate pathway from the genitals that they were looking for: the vagus nerve. They found that sexual stimulation bypassed the spinal cord and went directly from the genitals to the brain via the vagus nerve. Nerves from the mammary glands, uterus, and skin, especially the skin of the chest, also connect directly to this sensory superhighway. These vagal signals stimulated the brain's reward, emotion, and memory systems, causing the release of oxytocin, as well as exciting dopamine and rewarding opioids.

Evidently, the vagus is the conduit for many of the sensations that increase arousal and lead to orgasm—as well as for the full-tummy sensations that lead us to stop eating. It's not clear whether eating and sex use exactly the same nerves to tingle the brain's reward center, but they're pretty darned close. It makes perfect sense that we turn to food when we're lonely. To the brain, a pint of chunky fudge ice cream looks an awful lot like great sex.

eat for comfort

The trick in eating to comfort yourself is to eat enough fat to supply the oxytocin you crave without eating so much that your health suffers. Unfortunately, there's no research showing how much fat it takes to trigger the release of leptin and CCK (Blevins 2008). In one study, women drank 7 ounces of cream to produce leptin—way more than you should consume. Another small study found CCK release with just 25 grams of fat, or slightly less than an ounce (Froehlich, Gonvers, and Fried 1995). Dietary theories seem to come and go in waves. We've moved through the high-carb era and the fat-free phase into the low-carb epoch, which will probably be supplanted by still another theory. But science shows that, when it comes to being satisfied, we need all three nutrient groups. If you've eschewed fat, it's time to allow some back into your diet. If you've gone the low-carbohydrate route, add some in, especially at those times when you're eating for comfort.

This brings us to ice cream—and, unfortunately, to all the conventional wisdom about eating well and wisely. It's clear that ice cream, that supreme solace of the lonely and sad, works its magic, at least in part, by triggering an oxytocin release in your brain that may be similar to what you'd experience if you were with someone you loved. So, go for it! But go for it in moderation.

If you plan to soothe yourself with ice cream, choose a flavor that includes nuts, which will give you added protein; remember, a mix of protein, carbohydrate, and fat is more likely to satisfy you. Read the nutritional information on the container, and measure out an amount that will provide no more than 400 calories; don't eat out of the container. If it's hard to stop, try eating a hard-boiled egg first. This will fill your stomach and add protein. To maximize your pleasure, do nothing but eat: watching television will distract you from the good taste and nice feeling of the creamy goodness going down your throat.

If ice cream isn't your passion or you want to wean yourself away from it, there's a wide variety of foods you can select to satisfy your stomach and brain. Most of them offer a better array of nutrients, too. If you love chocolate, add a handful of almonds. A grilled cheese sandwich with tomatoes on multigrain bread should do the trick; so should a tuna-fish or egg-salad sandwich with real mayonnaise. Now that you know the physiological process leading to satiety, you can experiment to find foods you may not crave in themselves but that will give you the *feeling* you crave.

The ideal comfort-eating session might go like this: you spend fifteen minutes in your connection spot, if you have one. If not, sit quietly for fifteen minutes in a comfy chair as you think about how good your snack will be. Decide exactly what and how much you'll eat. Then, get up, prepare your meal, and bring it back to this spot where you've just experienced a bit of relaxation. Concentrate on every bite, savoring it as much as you can.

Love Yourself

Before we say good-bye to the vagus nerve, let's talk more about sex—specifically, the kind of sex you have with yourself. As we've seen, nature designed sex to be enjoyable and healthy. The release of oxytocin at orgasm benefits you no matter where that orgasm came from. If you don't have a trusted and trustworthy sex partner, consider masturbation. Like intercourse, masturbation to orgasm produces an oxytocin release in both women and men (Carmichael et al. 1994; Blaicher et al. 1999). Lots of people find it easier to orgasm through masturbation than through sexual intercourse. Certainly, when you pleasure yourself, you can do exactly what you like without worrying about pleasing the other person. There may also be less embarrassment: you're free from the distraction of how you look, sound, or smell. Unfortunately, when we talk about masturbation—and we seldom do—it tends to be treated as shameful, embarrassing, or a less desirable alternative to the "real thing."

But if you're struggling a bit with love relationships, loving yourself is an outstanding alternative to suffering from skin hunger or "hooking up." Regularly offering yourself this opportunity for an oxytocin release will soothe you and possibly keep you away from less healthy alternatives like overeating. It can also lower your susceptibility to falling into a romance with someone who can't offer you the commitment of oxytocin-based love.

Sometimes, a lack of safe, caring touch when we were younger, as well as violent or inappropriate touch during that period, made it difficult or impossible to achieve orgasm. Learning to masturbate to orgasm and enjoy the oxytocin release in private is a good first step toward eventual physical and emotional intimacy with someone else.

Things to Do in Groups

In addition to living in a family, human beings are highly social animals who thrive in groups. The need for society, or contact with many other people, is part of our nature. Although modern society tends to be organized around the nuclear family, you can look to groups for activities that amplify your oxytocin release as an alternative or adjunct to one-on-one interactions.

Church as Community

At 8:49 a.m. on a Saturday in late September, Sacramento's ARCO Arena is not a pretty place. The cold fluorescent light washes out the skin's pink and gold, casting harsh shadows on the faces of the five thousand women assembled here. But there's nothing chilly about the way they sway, eyes closed, the palms of their hands open and turned toward the sky like heat-seeking antennae. They're all singing the same song, a Christian paean of longing and admiration. Most of these women are in their mid-thirties or older; they've paid forty-five dollars and traveled from northern California, Oregon, and even Montana to spend three days at Contagious Joy, a conference that's a specifically feminine expression of spirituality.

While the songs praise the Lord, the motivational speakers focus on the quotidian trials of modern life: broken refrigerators, lost cell phones, quirky husbands, rambunctious kids. They put God in a context that's especially familiar and comfortable for women, with their focus on personal connection. He's the ideal husband and father: He loves them just the way they are, and he wants a personal relationship with each of them.

When people talk about having "a personal relationship with my savior," they often describe the relationship as sparking the same kinds of feelings as a loving relationship with another human. People who worship God or another such being engage in what sociologists call *para-social affiliation*, in other words, a relationship with a concept, character, or famous person that invokes the same feelings as does a relationship with another person (Horton and Wohl 1956). There's no research on the neurochemistry of religious feeling, but because we seem to use the same attachment and connection circuits for a wide variety of social interactions, it may be that feeling connected to God offers an oxytocin release. You don't need to worship to get these benefits. Nondenominational churches, as well as other kinds of groups that intentionally gather together, offer similar chances for connection to something greater than yourself. These include neighborhood associations, charities, and clubs.

Tend and Befriend

The Contagious Joy women know a secret: not only God but also other women can get you high. Remember Shelly Taylor's tend and befriend theory, the feminine alternative to the fight-or-flight response (Taylor 2000)? Taylor and her colleagues realized that while fight or flight is the primary response to stress for both sexes, in times of danger or fear, women instinctively move to gather the family together and protect their children. Because of this, women tend to form the kinds of social networks that provide mutual support and assistance. This is a pattern seen throughout the monogamous mammals: prairie voles huddle together, and chimpanzees will nurse a relative's baby. Taylor's hypothesis is that the oxytocin released in times of stress interacts with estrogen and natural opiates in the brain to drive women toward their friends in times of need.

While tend and befriend may be an instinct, Contagious Joy is a very conscious version. These women know they'll spend two days in a safe place in which they can befriend others who share their values. You can do the same thing in a number of ways: invite friends over to watch a comedy, sign up for a weekend retreat that expresses your values or interests, or join a women's organization dedicated to community work.

Sing it Up

Spiritual gatherings use a powerful technique to raise oxytocin levels and elevate the spirit: singing. In a study of professional and amateur singers at Stockholm's National Institute for Psychosocial Factors and Health, eight amateur vocalists experienced an oxytocin boost after a half-hour choral lesson (Grape et al. 2003). The women in the study also lowered their levels of cortisol.

The men's cortisol levels went up, however; this may have been due to performance anxiety. In any case, both sexes reported increasing joy and elatedness, more energy, and a mellower outlook after belting out a few numbers. The elements of singing are perfect for bringing a group into limbic resonance, that state where their autonomic nervous systems are attuned. First, there's the physical mirroring. As singers face the conductor or leader, they assume a similar posture. Their voices match each other's tone, pace, and volume. They breathe in unison. And the sound waves of their combined voices bathe their bodies and cause their eardrums to vibrate to the same frequencies. It's no wonder that they become so deeply attuned that they feel as if they're one body, one voice—and that they release oxytocin in response to this close connection.

We're not all singers, but we can be chanters, dancers, marchers, or drummers. While it's not certain that every group activity induces an oxytocin release, any activity that allows you to enter into limbic resonance with others helps satisfy the human need for connection.

Hugging Allowed

Cuddling with someone you feel close to and comfortable with seems like a reliable way to enjoy some oxytocin. But almost everyone goes through a period where hugs are hard to find. Two young urbanites decided to solve that problem with Cuddle Parties. In 2004, Reid Mihalko, a massage therapist and relationship counselor, and Marcia Baczynski, a sex educator and relationship coach, began hosting small get-togethers in Mihalko's New York apartment. Soon, there were Cuddle Parties every weekend, and more in California. Now, three years later, there are parties across the United States and in Toronto.

To attend a Cuddle Party, you show up in pajamas, pay a fee of thirty dollars or so, and lounge around on cushions. The rules are clear: first of all, no sex—of any kind. Pajamas stay on the whole time. And you have to ask and receive a verbal yes before touching anyone else. The idea of these boundaries is to keep the atmosphere snuggly, and to make sure no one has to worry about unwanted advances. At a Cuddle Party, people are encouraged to move around and cuddle with as many people as they want; they're also encouraged to say no whenever they want. They're advised to check in frequently with fellow cuddlers: "Is this okay? Does this feel good?"

I attended a Cuddle Party in Emeryville, California. About fifteen people gathered at the cheery, clean apartment, where an assortment of large cushions supplemented the comfy couch. We sat and got an orientation from the facilitator, and then, to break the ice, we did a "cow topple." Those of us who wanted to got down on our hands and knees, shoulder to shoulder. With a word from the facilitator, we leaned to the right until we fell over in a pile. Suddenly, we were cuddling.

Not everyone at this event was interested in serious cuddling though; a few people were quite wary. Why go to a Cuddle Party if you don't want to cuddle? Actually, the structured format is an excellent way to practice setting boundaries and saying no. This is great practice, especially for women who've been taught to be compliant or to take care of others.

During the three hours of the party, people moved in and out of groups. There were some shoulder massages, some foot rubs, spooning, and cradling. While some men shied away from he-to-he cuddling, most engaged in some comradely contact. Women, trained by society as the snuggling sex, were omnivorous cuddlers. Maybe that's why, on www.cuddleparty.com, Mihalko reports that he gets twice as many queries from men as from women. They try to maintain an even number of men and women at each party, and he says that, for most events, there are more men than women who want to come.

Mihalko and Baczynski seem to have hit on a need that isn't fulfilled in our culture, the simple need for friendly touch. They've designed their events to let even complete strangers exchange a little oxytocin in a safe and pleasant way.

Oxytocin at Work

Snuggly mommy love, comfy marriage—so far, we've looked at oxytocin in the human equivalent of nesting. Does oxytocin play a part in the workplace? You bet it does. Hugging and kissing may be taboo at work, but oxytocin exchanges are all over the place. That's because oxytocin also facilitates trust, and trust is at the root of all economic and social decisions.

It begins the minute you walk through the glass doors for your first job interview. If you listen to recruiters' advice with an ear for neurochemistry, you realize that they're talking about playing to the manager's social brain. On an interview, you're advised to try to establish a personal relationship quickly, use eye contact and friendly body language, and let your personality shine through. While the hiring manager's executive brain functions may be analyzing your résumé, her limbic system is engaging in unconscious friend-or-foe decision making.

After you've landed the position, your new colleagues are making unconscious decisions about your trustworthiness, as a coworker and as a potential friend. Where will you fit into the social hierarchy? Are you available for bitch sessions, or are you the type who tattles to the boss? Are you open to talking about your family, your hopes and dreams? Will you be nice to them?

When you do something to build a little bridge toward a coworker, his danger-sensing amygdala processes that information and tags you "maybe not foe." Enough nice gestures and helpful actions, and his social brain recognizes you as "friend," at least in the context of the workplace. If the relationship extends to after-work socializing, his social memory may put you in the smaller class of friends with whom it's possible to achieve limbic resonance.

Even if you don't develop deep friendships at work, being open to genuine connection during business hours seems to exercise the same brain circuits that we use to bond with a mate. Paul Zak, an economics professor at Claremont Graduate University in California, describes trust as "a temporary human attachment" (Zak 2005, 368). Zak is one of a handful of researchers who has administered oxytocin to people in controlled experiments. He's shown that the exchange of friendly social signals releases trust-building oxytocin (2005), and also that giving people oxytocin makes them more generous (Zak, Stanton, and Ahmadi 2007).

Zak is a pioneer in the new field of *neuroeconomics*, which applies neuroscience to human behavior in economic exchanges. He calls oxytocin the human race's "social glue," because he believes it's at the root of all trusting interactions (Zak 2007). And a trusting environment is not only good for people; it's good for business, he says.

What this means for you on the job is that you have the opportunity, through trusting interactions and collaboration, to engage in temporary attachments that have a twofold benefit. First, you can experience a mild oxytocin release that will keep your nervous system tuned up and your stress level lower. Second, you're likely to do your job better. Your better performance plus the connections you forge at work can help you succeed in your career as you strengthen your oxytocin response.

Things to Do One on One

In the continuum from building the oxytocin response on your own through practicing in groups, we now come to the ways you can grow the oxytocin response in one-to-one interactions. You can consciously deepen your connection to a friend, lover, or family member. If you're not ready to face the potential for drama or heartbreak inherent in romantic relationships, you also can enjoy the "temporary attachments" of exchanging care with a stranger.

Enjoy Therapeutic Touch

It seems logical that the rhythmic stroking of massage would provoke the oxytocin response, but as yet there are no studies in humans showing this result. Kerstin Uvnäs Moberg (2003), the scientist who first identified the power of oxytocin for healing and connection, showed that rhythmic stroking induced the oxytocin response in animals, and other researchers have replicated this effect.

One of Paul Zak's experiments seems to show that getting a massage might make us more open to connection. In 2008, Zak and his Claremont colleagues devised an experiment to see if being touched would make people more cooperative (Morhenn et al. 2008). Before they played a game in which they transferred money to each other, half the subjects spent time alone in a room. The other half enjoyed a fifteen-minute chair massage by a licensed massage therapist. Zak assumed the massage would boost oxytocin levels in the people who got the rub. It didn't. However, when the newly kneaded began to play the game, their brains did begin to pump out oxytocin when someone trusted them—and they were more generous than the control group. Zak hypothesizes that the chair massage acted as a signal that primed study participants for trust and generosity.

Another way of saying this is that massage makes us more relaxed, and when we're relaxed, we tend to be more open to others. Massage also has proven physiological benefits, including lowering blood pressure and heart rate, reducing cortisol levels, and decreasing pain—all properties of oxytocin (Uvnäs Moberg 2003). To get the most oxytocin-producing benefits, choose a gentle, soothing massage style. Avoid deep-tissue work or hard acupressure; while these are valuable techniques for reducing muscle tension, their intensity may not allow for the right kind of relaxation. The Swedish or Esalen styles use gentler, rhythmic motions that have been shown to elevate oxytocin levels in animals. After the massage, you can test whether you feel more open to connection by calling or visiting with a friend.

Keep the Home Fires Burning

If you're lucky enough to have a mate, he or she becomes one of your most reliable sources of oxytocin. As we saw in chapter 4, sex and orgasm stimulate a powerful release of oxytocin that calms the body and reinforces the bond. Sex does indeed make love.

Unfortunately, in a long-term relationship, due to habit and the pressures of daily life, sex may come to be seen by both halves of the couple as the man's reward for good behavior, instead of the very wellspring of the bond between them. There are often physiological differences in a man's and woman's desires because of his greater levels of testosterone. This difference may have been reinforced by habit. When the relationship was in the extremely exciting romantic phase, her sexual response may have been as rapid as his; she needed fewer signals to become aroused, and she was ready for intercourse as quickly as he was. Now that they enjoy the familiarity of sleeping beside each other every night, she may require a much longer period of touching before she's excited enough for penetration, while he's become used to quickly moving on to the main event.

If they become parents, both of them may focus their deepest affections on the children. As we've seen, this is essential to a great extent, in order for the children to survive and thrive. And, of course, a new mother's brain and body are primed by oxytocin and the other neurochemicals of labor and birth to cause her to give herself completely to her newborn. For many couples, however, the arrival of a baby puts an end to their exuberant sex life.

As the two move into their thirties and forties, his testosterone levels drop. He may experience erectile dysfunction and, unfortunately, feel shame that causes him to avoid lovemaking. Her lubrication may lessen as her estrogen levels also ebb, making sex painful. Meanwhile, jobs, kids, and all the other challenges of daily life stress them out. A stressed-out person finds it more difficult to activate the parasympathetic nervous system and enjoy the oxytocin response. When you're too tweaked out to settle into your calm spot, sex—specifically, an orgasm—can act as your reset button.

There are myriad books and magazine articles with excellent advice on how to bring hot sex back into your relationship. Most of them emphasize that you have to make time to have sex, even if that means the somewhat unromantic method of making an appointment. You can also learn to make daily reconnections that reinforce the oxytocin bond you have.

Help Someone or Something

As we've seen, mothering seems to prime the brain to be more sensitive to oxytocin. While much of this effect should be attributed to the profound hormonal changes of pregnancy, the brains of fathers, too, undergo changes that must be due to behavior and the family environment. It could be that, while oxytocin makes us more generous, giving to others or caring for someone or something also primes us to become more sensitive to the connecting effects of oxytocin. You can find opportunities to care for others by volunteering at organizations of all kinds. You can limit your commitment to what feels doable, while you slowly expand your comfort zone and raise the temperature on your emotional thermostat.

Let Someone Help You

People like me, the tough-it-out crowd, feel that it's wrong to burden others with our problems: "Maybe she won't like me if she finds out I'm not perfect," we think. "He'll be annoyed that I asked for help." "I hate to impose." Even if you don't naturally look to others for an emotional boost, understanding the oxytocin response can relieve those fears. Healthy people like to help others; they get their own oxytocin burst when they give support, and this makes them like someone they help even more.

For a couple of years, I worked near a little Mediterranean deli in San Francisco. The food was interesting, healthy, and reasonably priced, so I went there two or three times a week. The two women who worked behind the counter were pleasant enough. But the day I forgot my wallet marked a turning point in our relationship. I'd heaped my plate with an assortment of food from the buffet table and carried it to the cash register when I realized my mistake. My office was three blocks away; I could easily have left the plate at the register while I retrieved my wallet. But these nice women insisted that I take the food and pay for it next time I came in.

Their trust certainly made me feel good, but what was really interesting was how it changed *their* behavior toward *me*. Of course, they were happy to see me come in again with the money, but they remained happy to see me on my future visits—happier than before the wallet incident. They had trusted me and helped me, I had repaid their trust, and now they were my friends. Paul Zak's experiments (Zak, Kurzban, and Matzner 2005) have shown how this kind of trusting exchange increases oxytocin levels in the participants. We now had a bond.

It can seem so impossible to reach out and ask a friend, an acquaintance, or, especially, a stranger for aid. Next time you shy away from asking, remind yourself that you're actually offering that person a chance for his or her own oxytocin hit—and dare to do it.

The Future: Oxytocin as a Drug

If you feel so at a loss in social situations that you wonder if your brain produces the oxytocin response at all, there may soon be drugs that can help you. In the near future, doctors will use oxytocin-based pharmaceuticals, or drugs with an artificial form of oxytocin, to treat social phobia. Clinical trials are already under way that use oxytocin to treat some of the symptoms of autism spectrum disorders (ASDs) (Quay 2007). A small study of adults with ASDs showed an intriguing result: not only were the people in the study better able to pick up on the emotional expression in speech, but the effects lasted for weeks after the dose of oxytocin (Hollander et al. 2006). Another study is examining whether oxytocin could be used in psychotherapy to give people a taste of what it's like to feel connected (University of New South Wales 2007). When these drugs reach the market, it's possible that they'll become as widely used as antidepressants now are. In the meantime, remember that you have the power to change your brain using the techniques in this chapter.

conclusion

Oxytocin brings balance and health to your physiological state. While the closeness of a mate and a family can create the calm and connection we need, there are many other ways you can evoke the oxytocin response. We're always being told we should relax. In chapter 7, we discussed several things you can do by yourself to relax, that is, to signal your parasympathetic nervous system that it's time for it to begin its good work. If you make a time and place for yourself to engage in a miniretreat every day, you'll soon learn to evoke the oxytocin response whenever you need to.

We also looked at how oxytocin is the basis of everyday relationships at work and in the community. Just as we're hardwired for intimacy, we're also hardwired for sociability. Those monogamous prairie voles also benefit from the company of individuals besides their mates. In the laboratory, housing pairs of females together relieves the stress they feel at isolation (Grippo, Cushing, and Carter 2007). You, too, can benefit from the company of other people, even strangers. You may say, "I'm not a joiner." But now that you understand how your physiology responds to the company of others, you can find some activity that lets you cooperate with others.

I wrote this book to show how science has illuminated the central mystery of human existence: how we love—or why we can't. Understanding how oxytocin creates the deep bonds of love, and why love is so important for not only our emotional lives but also our health, proves that the emphasis people have always placed on love is not merely romantic or idealistic. Love, defined as the oxytocin bond, is indeed central to our well-being. Therefore, we need to ignore those directives of society or our own hearts that tell us to be strong and tough, that we should be able to go it alone. Finding love becomes central to our life's work.

I also wanted to reveal a secret that's been hidden in plain sight: we're not born knowing how to love. We learn the oxytocin response from those who take care of us as babies. In the critical first three years of life, our innate capacity to love deeply may be nurtured and thrive. But it may also be thwarted, twisted, or choked off. If the oxytocin response doesn't develop in a healthy way, we may spend our whole lives alone—or in abusive or unsatisfying relationships. We may get stuck in the romance stage, moving from one passionate adventure to the next, wondering why this kind of "love" always ends.

If you struggle with relationships, you may feel as if there's something wrong with you. Maybe you feel guilty that you can't reciprocate the affection that others offer. You may feel especially bad when you date someone who's clearly falling in love with you. You don't want to hurt anyone, and you hope that maybe this time will be different. But there always comes the point when you have to say, "I just don't love you." And then you feel as if you're a bad person. You may feel ashamed that you don't have the kind of love relationships you see other people enjoying.

If that's you, simply knowing that your oxytocin response was formed long before you were able to make any conscious choices can bring a lot of relief. You can reflect on how the kind of love you got, or its lack, is recreated over and over in your adult life. More important, as this book has shown, you have the power to change the way you love for the better. This book explains how it's possible to learn the oxytocin response, even late in life, by consciously recreating the experiences that should've trained your neurochemical reactions when you were just a baby.

Now that you understand the oxytocin response, you can kindle its spark and carefully train it to flower inside your own brain so that you can freely give and accept the love we all deserve.

references

Adam, E. K., L. C. Hawkley, B. M. Kudielka, and J. T. Cacioppo. 2006. Day-to-day dynamics of experience: Cortisol associations in a population-based sample of older adults. *Proceedings of the National Academy of Sciences* 103 (45):17058–63.

Adolphs, R., D. Tranel, and A. R. Damasio. 1998. The human amygdala in social judgment. *Nature* 393 (6684):470–74.

Akman, I., K. Kusçu, N. Özdemir, Z. Yurdakul, M. Solakoglu, L. Orhan, A. Karabekiroglu, and E. Özek. 2006. Mothers' postpartum psychological adjustment and infantile colic. *Archives of Diseases in Childhood* 91:417–19.

Allen, K. M., J. Blascovich, J. Tomaka, and R. M. Kelsey. 1991. Presence of human friends and pet dogs as moderators of autonomic responses to stress in women. *Journal of Personality and Social Psychology* 61 (4):582–89.

American Psychiatric Association. 2000. *Diagnostic and Statistical Manual of Mental Disorders.* 4th ed., text rev. Arlington, VA: American Psychiatric Association.

Aragona, B. J., Y. Liu, J. T. Curtis, F. K. Stephan, and Z. X. Wang. 2003. A critical role for nucleus accumbens dopamine in partner-preference formation in male prairie voles. *Journal of Neuroscience* 23 (8):3483–90.

Aragona, B. J., Y. Liu, Y. J. Yu, J. T. Curtis, J. M. Detwiler, T. R. Insel, and Z. Wang. 2006. Nucleus accumbens dopamine differentially mediates the formation and maintenance of monogamous pair-bonds. *Nature Neuroscience* 9 (1):133–39.

Argiolas, A., and M. R. Melis. 2004. The role of oxytocin and the paraventricular nucleus in the sexual behaviour of male mammals. *Physiology and Behavior* 83 (2):309–17.

Aron, P. A., H. E. Fisher, D. J. Mashek, G. Strong, H. Li, and L. L. Brown. 2005. Reward, motivation, and emotion systems associated with early-stage intense romantic love. *Journal of Neurophysiology* 94 (1):327–37.

Bale, T. L., A. M. Davis, A. P. Auger, D. M. Dorsa, and M. M. McCarthy. 2001. CNS region-specific oxytocin receptor expression: Importance in regulation of anxiety and sex behavior. *Journal of Neuroscience* 21 (7):2546–52.

Bales, K. L. 2007. Interview by author. April 13. Davis, CA.

Bales, K. L., and C. S. Carter. 2003. Developmental exposure to oxytocin facilitates partner preferences in male prairie voles (*Microtus ochrogaster*). *Behavioral Neuroscience* 117 (4):854–59.

Bales, K. L., A. J. Kim, A. D. Lewis-Reese, and C. S. Carter. 2004. Both oxytocin and vasopressin may influence alloparental behavior in male prairie voles. *Hormones and Behavior* 45 (5):354–61.

Bales, K. L., A. D. Lewis-Reese, L. Pfeifer, K. Kramer, and C. S. Carter. 2007a. Early experience affects the traits of monogamy in a sexually dimorphic manner. *Developmental Psychobiology* 49 (4):335–42.

Bales, K. L., W. A. Mason, C. Catana, S. R. Cherry, and S. P. Mendoza. 2007b. Neural correlates of pair-bonding in a monogamous primate. *Brain Research* 1184:245–53.

Bartels, A., and S. Zeki. 2000. The neural basis of romantic love. *NeuroReport* 11 (17):3829–34.

———. 2004. The neural correlates of maternal and romantic love. *NeuroImage* 21 (3):1155–66.

Bealer, S. L., D. L. Lipschitz, G. Ramoz, and W. R. Crowley. 2006. Oxytocin receptor binding in the hypothalamus during gestation in rats. *American Journal of Physiology: Regulatory Integrative and Comparative Physiology* 291:53–58.

Beauregard, M., J. Lévesque, and P. Bourgouin. 2001. Neural correlates of conscious self-regulation of emotion. *Journal of Neuroscience* 21:RC165:1–6.

Beaver, J. D., A. D. Lawrence, J. van Ditzhuijzen, M. H. Davis, A. Woods, and A. J. Calder. 2006. Individual differences in reward drive predict neural responses to images of food. *The Journal of Neuroscience* 26 (19):5160–66.

Bellis, M. A., J. Downing, and J. R. Ashton. 2006. Adults at 12? Trends in puberty and their public health consequences. *Journal of Epidemiology and Community Health* 60:910–11.

Berglund, H., P. Lindström, and I. Savic. 2006. Brain response to putative pheromones in lesbian women. *Proceedings of the National Academy of Sciences* 103 (21):8269–74.

Bermant, G., D. F. Lott, and L. Anderson. 1968. Temporal characteristics of the Coolidge effect in male rat copulatory behavior. *Journal of Comparative and Physiological Psychology* 65 (3):447–52.

Bernhardt, P. C., J. M. Dabbs, Jr., J. A. Fielden, and C. D. Lutter. 1998. Testosterone changes during vicarious experiences of winning and losing among fans at sporting events. *Physiology and Behavior* 65 (1):59–62.

Bernier, A., S. Larose, M. Boivin, and N. Soucy. 2004. Attachment state of mind: Implications for adjustment to college. *Journal of Adolescent Research* 19 (6):783–806.

Blaicher, W., D. Gruber, C. Bieglmayer, A. M. Blaicher, W. Knogler, and J. C. Huber. 1999. The role of oxytocin in relation to female sexual arousal. *Gynecologic and Obstetric Investigation* 47 (2):125–26.

Blevins, J. E. 2008. E-mail interview by author. May 20.

Blevins J. E., T. J. Eakin, J. A. Murphy, M. W. Schwartz, and D. G. Baskin. 2003. Oxytocin innervation of caudal brainstem nuclei activated by cholecystokinin. *Brain Research* 993 (1–2):30–41.

Blevins, J. E., B. G. Truong, and D. W. Gietzen. 2004. NMDA receptor function within the anterior piriform cortex and lateral hypothalamus in rats on the control of intake of amino acid-deficient diets. *Brain Research* 1019 (1–2):124–33.

Bowlby, J. 1990. *A Secure Base: Parent-Child Attachment and Healthy Human Development*. New York: Basic Books.

Brizendine, L. 2006. *The Female Brain*. New York: Morgan Road Books.

Brumbaugh, C. C., and R. C. Fraley. 2007. The transference of attachment patterns: How parental and romantic relationships influence feelings toward novel people. *Personal Relationships* 14 (4):513–30.

Cacioppo, J. T. 2007. Interview by author. February 16. Chicago.

Cacioppo, J. T., J. M. Ernst, M. H. Burleson, M. K. McClintock, W. B. Malarkey, L. C. Hawkley, R. B. Kowalewski, A. Paulsen, J. A. Hobson, K. Hugdahl, D. Spiegel, and G. G. Berntson. 2000. Lonely traits and concomitant physiological processes: The MacArthur Social Neuroscience Studies. *International Journal of Psychophysiology* 35 (2–3):143–54.

Cacioppo, J. T., and L. C. Hawkley. 2005. People thinking about people: The vicious cycle of being a social outcast in one's own mind. In *The Social Outcast: Ostracism, Social Exclusion, Rejection, and Bullying*, ed. K. D. Williams, J. P. Forgas, and W. von Hippel. New York: Psychology Press, 91–108.

Cacioppo, J. T., M. E. Hughes, L. J. Waite, L. C. Hawkley, and R. A. Thisted. 2006. Loneliness as a specific risk factor for depressive symptoms: Cross-sectional and longitudinal analyses. *Psychology and Aging* 21 (1):140–51.

Cacioppo, J. T., C. J. Norris, J. Decety, G. Monteleone, and H. Nusbaum. Forthcoming. In the eye of the beholder: Individual differences in perceived social isolation predict regional brain activation to social stimuli. *Journal of Cognitive Neuroscience*.

Carmichael, M. S., V. L. Warburton, J. Dixen, and J. M. Davidson. 1994. Relationships among cardiovascular, muscular, and oxytocin responses during human sexual activity. *Archives of Sexual Behavior* 23 (1):59–79.

Carter, C. S. 2007a. Sex differences in oxytocin and vasopressin: Implications for autism spectrum disorders? *Behavioural Brain Research* 176 (1):170–86.

———. 2007b. Interview by author. February 19. Chicago.

Carter, C. S., A. C. DeVries, and L. L. Getz. 1995. Physiological substrates of mammalian monogamy: The prairie vole model. *Neuroscience and Biobehavioral Reviews* 19 (2):303–14.

Champagne, F. A., P. Chretien, C. W. Stevenson, T. Y. Zhang, A. Gratton, and M. J. Meaney. 2004. Variations in nucleus accumbens dopamine associated with individual differences in maternal behavior in the rat. *The Journal of Neuroscience* 24 (17):4113–23.

Champagne, F. A., J. Diorio, S. Sharma, and M. J. Meaney. 2001. Naturally occurring variations in maternal behavior in the rat are associated with differences in estrogen-inducible central oxytocin receptors. *Proceedings of the National Academy of Sciences* 98 (22):12736–41.

Cho, M. M., A. C. DeVries, J. R. Williams, and C. S. Carter. 1999. The effects of oxytocin and vasopressin on partner preferences in male and female prairie voles (*Microtus ochrogaster*). *Behavioral Neuroscience* 113 (5):1071–79.

Chung, W. C. J., G. J. De Vries, and D. F. Swaab. 2002. Sexual differentiation of the bed nucleus of the stria terminalis in humans may extend into adulthood. *Journal of Neuroscience* 22 (3):1027–33.

Clark, S. 2007. Interview by author. May 15. Albany, CA.

Cozolino, L. 2002. *The Neuroscience of Psychotherapy: Building and Rebuilding the Human Brain.* New York: W. W. Norton & Co., Inc.

Cushing, B. S., and C. S. Carter. 1999. Prior exposure to oxytocin mimics the effects of social contact and facilitates sexual behaviour in females. *Journal of Neuroendocrinology* 11 (10):765–69.

Ditzen, B., G. Bodenmann, U. Ehlert, and M. Heinrichs. 2006. Effects of social support and oxytocin on psychological and physiological stress responses during marital conflict. *Frontiers in Neuroendocrinology* 27 (1):134.

Doidge, N. 2007. *The Brain That Changes Itself: Stories of Personal Triumph from the Frontiers of Brain Science.* New York: Penguin Books.

Etkin, A., M. Phil, C. Pittenger, H. J. Polan, and E. R. Kandel. 2005. Toward a neurobiology of psychotherapy: Basic science and clinical applications. *Journal of Neuropsychiatry and Clinical Neurosciences* 17:145–58.

Evans, J. J. 1997. Oxytocin in the human: Regulation of derivations and destinations. *European Journal of Endocrinology* 137 (6):559–71.

Feldman, R., A. Weller, O. Zagoory-Sharon, and A. Levine. 2007. Evidence for a neuroendocrinological foundation of human affiliation: Plasma oxytocin levels across pregnancy and the postpartum period predict maternal-infant bonding. *Psychological Science* 18 (11):965–70.

Fisher, H. E. 1998. Lust, attraction, and attachment in mammalian reproduction. *Human Nature* 9 (1):23–52.

———. 2004. *Why We Love: The Nature and Chemistry of Romantic Love.* New York: Henry Holt and Company, LLC.

Fisher, H. E., A. Aron, and L. L. Brown. 2006. Romantic love: A mammalian brain system for mate choice. *Philosophical Transactions of the Royal Society* 361 (1476):2173–86.

Fisher, H. E., A. Aron, D. Mashek, H. Li, and L. L. Brown. 2002. Defining the brain systems of lust, romantic attraction, and attachment. *Archives of Sexual Behavior* 31 (5):413–19.

Fraley, R. C., and P. R. Shaver. 2000. Adult romantic attachment: Theoretical developments, emerging controversies, and unanswered questions. *Review of General Psychology 2000* 4 (2):132–54.

Friedmann, E. 1991. The role of pets in enhancing human well-being: Physiological effects. In *The Waltham Book of Human-Animal Interaction: Benefits and Responsibilities of Pet Ownership*, ed. I. Robinson. London: Pergamon Press.

Froehlich, F., J. J. Gonvers, and M. Fried. 1995. Role of nutrient fat and cholecystokinin in regulation of gallbladder emptying in man. *Digestive diseases and sciences* 40 (3):529–33.

Furness, J. B. 2006. The organisation of the autonomic nervous system: Peripheral connections. *Autonomic Neuroscience* 130 (1–2):1–5.

Geary, D. C., and M. V. Flinn. 2002. Sex differences in behavioral and hormonal response to social threat: Commentary on Taylor et al. *Psychological Review* 109 (4):745–50.

Georgiadis, J. R., R. Kortekaas, R. Kuipers, A. Nieuwenburg, J. Pruim, A. A. T. S. Reinders, and G. Holstege. 2006. Regional cerebral blood flow changes associated with clitorally induced orgasm in healthy women. *European Journal of Neuroscience* 24 (11):3305–16.

Gimpl, G., and F. Fahrenholz. 2001. The oxytocin receptor system: Structure, function, and regulation. *Physiological Reviews* 81 (2):629–83.

Grape, C., M. Sandgren, L. O. Hansson, M. Ericson, and T. Theorell. 2003. Does singing promote well-being? An empirical study of professional and amateur singers during a singing lesson. *Integrative Physiological and Behavioral Science* 38 (1):65–74.

Gray, P. B., B. C. Campbell, F. W. Marlowe, S. F. Lipson, and P. T. Ellison. 2004. Social variables predict between-subject but not day-to-day variation in the testosterone of U.S. men. *Psychoneuroendocrinology* 29 (9):1153–62.

Grewen, K. M., S. S. Girdler, J. Amico, and K. C. Light. 2005. Effects of partner support on resting oxytocin, cortisol, norepinephrine, and blood pressure before and after warm partner contact. *Psychosomatic Medicine* 67 (4):531–38.

Grewen K. M., S. S. Girdler, and K. C. Light. 2005. Relationship quality: Effects on ambulatory blood pressure and negative affect in a biracial sample of men and women. *Blood Pressure Monitoring* 10 (3):117–24.

Grippo, A. J., B. S. Cushing, and C. S. Carter. 2007. Depression-like behavior and stressor-induced neuroendocrine activation in female prairie voles exposed to chronic social isolation. *Psychosomatic Medicine* 69:149–57.

Gurian, M. 1996. *The Wonder of Boys: What Parents, Mentors, and Educators Can Do to Shape Boys into Exceptional Men*. New York: Jeremy P. Tarcher/Putnam.

———. 1998. *A Fine Young Man: What Parents, Mentors, and Educators Can Do to Shape Adolescent Boys into Exceptional Men*. New York: Jeremy P. Tarcher/Putnam.

———. 1999. *The Good Son: Shaping the Moral Development of Our Boys and Young Men*. New York: Jeremy P. Tarcher/Putnam.

———. 2007. Telephone interview by author. January 18.

Hammock, E. A. D., M. M. Lim, H. P. Nair, and L. J. Young. 2005. Association of vasopressin 1a receptor levels with a regulatory microsatellite and behavior. *Genes, Brain, and Behavior* 4 (5):289–301.

Hammock, E. A. D., and L. J. Young. 2005. Microsatellite instability generates diversity in brain and sociobehavioral traits. *Science* 308 (5728):1630–34.

Hawkley, L. C., and J. T. Cacioppo. 2007. Aging and loneliness: Downhill quickly? *Current Directions in Psychological Science* 16 (4):187–91.

Hawkley, L. C., C. M. Masi, J. D. Berry, and J. T. Cacioppo. 2006. Loneliness is a unique predictor of age-related differences in systolic blood pressure. *Psychology and Aging* 21 (1):152–64.

Heinrichs, M., T. Baumgartner, C. Kirschbaum, and U. Ehlert. 2003. Social support and oxytocin interact to suppress cortisol and subjective responses to psychosocial stress. *Biological Psychiatry* 54 (12):1389–98.

Herman-Giddens, M. E., E. J. Slora, R. C. Wasserman, C. J. Bourdony, M. V. Bhapkar, G. G. Koch, and C. M. Hasemeier. 1997. Secondary sexual characteristics and menses in young girls seen in office practice: A study from the Pediatric Research in Office Settings network. *Pediatrics* 99 (4):505–12.

Hoffman, K., R. Marvin, G. Cooper, and B. Powell. 2006. Changing toddlers' and preschoolers' attachment classifications: The Circle of Security intervention. *Journal of Consulting and Clinical Psychology* 74 (6):1017–26.

Holland, G. 2006. Hot sweaty sex: Investigating the ins and outs of human chemical communication. *Research Reporter* 27, newsletter of Brock University, St. Catharines, Ontario, Canada.

Hollander, E., J. Bartz, W. Chaplin, A. Phillips, J. Sumner, L. Soorya, E. Anagnostou, and S. Wasserman. 2006. Oxytocin increases retention of social cognition in autism. *Biological Psychiatry* 61 (4):498–503.

Holstege, G. 2007. Brain activity during male and female orgasms. Paper presented at Neurobiology of Love Conference, January 20, University of California at Berkeley.

Holstege, G., J. R. Georgiadis, A. M. J. Paans, L. C. Meiners, F. H. C. E. van der Graaf, and A. A. T. S. Reinders. 2003. Brain activation during human male ejaculation. *Journal of Neuroscience* 23 (27):9185–93.

Horton, D., and R. R. Wohl. 1956. Mass communication and para-social interaction: Observations on intimacy at a distance. *Psychiatry* 19 (3):215–29.

Hrdy, S. B. 1999. *Mother Nature: A History of Mothers, Infants, and Natural Selection.* New York: Pantheon Books.

Insel, T. R. 1997. A neurobiological basis of social attachment. *American Journal of Psychiatry* 154 (6):726–35.

Jackson, M. 2007. In J. Sakai, Study finds Viagra increases release of key reproductive hormone. EurekAlert, August 23. http://www.eurekalert .org/pub_releases/2007-08/uow-sfv082307.php (accessed August 25, 2008).

Jacobsen, T., and V. Hofmann. 1997. Children's attachment representations: Longitudinal relations to school behavior and academic competency in middle childhood and adolescence. *Developmental Psychology* 33 (4):703–10.

Jorgensen, H., M. Riis, U. Knigge, A. Kjaer, and J. Warberg. 2003. Serotonin receptors involved in vasopressin and oxytocin secretion. *Journal of Neuroendocrinology* 15 (3):242–49.

Kaplowitz, P. 2004. *Early Puberty in Girls: The Essential Guide to Coping with This Common Problem.* New York: Ballantine Books.

Kempenaers, B., G. R. Verheyen, M. van den Broeck, T. Burke, C. van Broeckhoven, and A. Dhondt. 1992. Extra-pair paternity results from female preference for high-quality males in the blue tit. *Nature* 357:494–96.

Kendrick, K. M. 2000. Oxytocin, motherhood, and bonding. *Experimental Physiology* 85 (Suppl. 1):111S–24S.

Kessler, R. C., P. A. Berglund, O. Demler, R. Jin, K. R. Merikangas, and E. E. Walters. 2005. Lifetime prevalence and age-of-onset distributions of *DSM-IV* disorders in the National Comorbidity Survey Replication (NCS-R). *Archives of General Psychiatry* 62 (6):593–602.

Kiecolt-Glaser, J. K., and T. L. Newton. 2001. Marriage and health: His and hers. *Psychological Bulletin* 127 (4):472–503.

Kirsch, P., C. Esslinger, Q. Chen, D. Mier, S. Lis, S. Siddhanti, H. Gruppe, V. S. Mattay, B. Gallhofer, and A. Meyer-Lindenberg. 2005. Oxytocin modulates neural circuitry for social cognition and fear in humans. *The Journal of Neuroscience* 25 (49):11489–93.

Klaus, M., and J. Kennell. 1983. *Bonding: The Beginnings of Parent-Infant Attachment.* New York: New American Library.

Kline, K. K., ed., and the Commission on Children at Risk. 2003. *Hardwired to Connect: The New Scientific Case for Authoritative Communities.* New York: Institute for American Values.

Komisaruk, B. R., C. Beyer-Flores, and B. Whipple. 2006. *The Science of Orgasm.* Baltimore: The Johns Hopkins University Press.

Komisaruk, B. R., and B. Whipple. 2005. Functional MRI of the brain during orgasm in women. *Annual Review of Sex Research* 16:62–86.

Kunz, G., D. Beil, P. Huppert, and G. Leyendecker. 2007. Oxytocin: A stimulator of directed sperm transport in humans. *Reproductive BioMedicine Online* 14 (1):32–39.

Larose, S., A. Bernier, and G. Tarabulsy. 2005. Attachment state of mind, learning dispositions, and academic performance during the college transition. *Developmental Psychology* 41 (1):281–89.

Levine, A., O. Zagoory-Sharon, R. Feldman, and A. Weller. 2007. Oxytocin during pregnancy and early postpartum: Individual patterns and maternal-fetal attachment. *Peptides* 28 (6):1162–69.

Liu, Y., and Z. X. Wang. 2003. Nucleus accumbens oxytocin and dopamine interact to regulate pair bond formation in female prairie voles. *Neuroscience* 121 (3):537–44.

Maestripieri, D. 2003. Similarities in affiliation and aggression between cross-fostered rhesus macaque females and their biological mothers. *Developmental Psychobiology* 43 (4):321–27.

———. 2005. Early experience affects the intergenerational transmission of infant abuse in rhesus monkeys. *Proceedings of the National Academy of Sciences* 102 (27):9726–29.

Mainous, R. O. 2002. Infant massage as a component of developmental care: Past, present, and future. *Holistic Nursing Practice* 17 (1):1–7.

Marazziti, D., H. S. Akiskal, A. Rossi, and G. B. Cassano. 1999. Alteration of the platelet serotonin transporter in romantic love. *Psychological Medicine* 29 (3):741–45.

Marazziti, D., and D. Canale. 2004. Hormonal changes when falling in love. *Psychoneuroendocrinology* 29 (7):931–36.

Marazziti, D., B. Dell'Osso, S. Baroni, F. Mungai, M. Catena, P. Rucci, F. Albanese, G. Giannaccini, L. Betti, L. Fabbrini, P. Italiani, A. del Debbio, A. Lucacchini, and L. Dell'Osso. 2006. A relationship between oxytocin and anxiety of romantic attachment. *Clinical Practice and Epidemiology in Mental Health* 2:28.

McKay, M., and P. Fanning. 2006. *The Daily Relaxer: Relax Your Body, Calm Your Mind, and Refresh Your Spirit.* Oakland, CA: New Harbinger Publications, Inc.

Mikulincer, M., and P. R. Shaver. 2007. *Attachment in Adulthood: Structure, Dynamics, and Change.* New York: The Guilford Press.

Moll, J., F. Krueger, R. Zahn, M. Pardini, R. de Oliveira-Souza, and J. Grafman. 2006. Human fronto-mesolimbic networks guide decisions about charitable donation. *Proceedings of the National Academy of Sciences* 103 (42):15623–28.

Morhenn, V. B., J. W. Park, E. Piper, and P. J. Zak. 2008. Monetary sacrifice among strangers is mediated by endogenous oxytocin release after physical contact. *Evolution and Human Behavior.* http://www.ehb online.org/article/S1090-5138(08)00048-2/abstract.

Murphy, M. R., J. R. Seckl, S. Burton, S. A. Checkley, and S. L. Lightman. 1987. Changes in oxytocin and vasopressin secretion during sexual activity in men. *Journal of Clinical Endocrinology and Metabolism* 65 (4):738–41.

Newport, F. 2007. Just Why Do Americans Attend Church? *Gallup News Service,* April 6. http://www.gallup.com/poll/27124/Just-Why-Americans-Attend-Church.aspx.

Nowak, R., A. P. Goursaud, F. Lévy, P. Orgeur, B. Schaal, C. Belzung, M. Picard, M. C. Meunier-Salaün, P. Alster, and K. Uvnäs Moberg. 1997. Cholecystokinin receptors mediate the development of a preference for the mother by newly born lambs. *Behavioral Neuroscience* 111 (6):1375–82.

Odendaal, J. S., and R. A. Meintjes. 2003. Neurophysiological correlates of affiliative behaviour between humans and dogs. *Veterinary Journal* 165 (3):296–301.

Perry, B. D. 2002. Childhood experience and the expression of genetic potential: What childhood neglect tells us about nature and nurture. *Brain and Mind* 3 (1):79–100.

Pert, C. 1997. *Molecules of Emotion: The Science Behind Mind-Body Medicine.* New York: Scribner.

Pfaus, J. G., and B. J. Everitt. 2000. The psychopharmacology of sexual behavior. In *Psychopharmacology: The Fourth Generation of Progress,* ed. F. Bloom and D. Kupfer. Philadelphia: Lippincott, Williams & Wilkins. http://www.acnp.org/g4/GN401000071/Default.htm.

Post, B. 2007. Telephone interview by author. May 27.

Powell, B. 2006. Telephone interview by author. October 15.

Quay, S. 2007. Telephone interview by author. April 9.

Rubinow, D. R., P. J. Schmidt, and C. A. Roca. 2002. Hormonal and gender influences on mood regulation. In *Neuropsychopharmacology: The Fifth Generation of Progress,* ed. K. L. Davis, D. Charney, J. T. Coyle, and C. B. Nemeroff, 1165–74. Philadelphia: Lippincott, Williams & Wilkins.

Russell, D. W. 1996. UCLA loneliness scale (version 3): Reliability, validity, and factor structure. *Journal of Personality Assessment* 66 (1):20–40.

Savic, I., H. Berglund, and P. Lindström. 2005. Brain response to putative pheromones in homosexual men. *Neuroscience* 102 (20):7356–61.

Sawahata, L., and K. Eldridge. 2007. *The Complete Color Harmony Workbook.* Gloucester, MA: Rockport Publishers.

Schore, A. N. 2003. *Affect Regulation and the Repair of the Self.* New York: W. W. Norton & Company, Inc.

———. 2007. Presentation at Children in Trauma conference, January 12–13, Chico State University, Chico, CA.

Schumacher, M., H. Coirini, D. W. Pfaff, and B. S. McEwen. 1990. Behavioral effects of progesterone associated with rapid modulation of oxytocin receptors. *Science* 250 (4981):691–94.

Shattuck, R. 1980. *The Forbidden Experiment: The Story of the Wild Boy of Aveyron*. New York: Farrar, Straus, and Giroux.

Siegel, D. J. 1999. *The Developing Mind: Toward a Neurobiology of Interpersonal Experience*. New York: The Guilford Press.

Smith, T. D., and K. P. Bhatnagar. 2000. The human vomeronasal organ. Part II: Prenatal development. *Journal of Anatomy* 197 (Pt. 3):421–36.

Taylor, S. E., L. C. Klein, B. P. Lewis, T. L. Gruenewald, R. A. Gurung, and J. A. Updegraff. 2000. Biobehavioral responses to stress in females: Tend-and-befriend, not fight-or-flight. *Psychological Review* 107 (3):411–29.

Thackare, H., H. D. Nicholson, and K. Whittington. 2006. Oxytocin: Its role in male reproduction and new potential therapeutic uses. *Human Reproduction Update* 12 (4):437–48.

Thompson, R. R., K. George, J. C. Walton, S. P. Orr, and J. Benson. 2006. Sex-specific influences of vasopressin on human social communication. *Proceedings of the National Academy of Sciences* 103 (20):7889–94.

Tronick, E. Z. 2002. A model of infant mood states and sandarian affective waves. *Psychoanalytic Dialogues* 12 (1):73–99.

University of New South Wales. 2007. Unleashing the love hormone. Press release, May 29. http://www.unsw.edu.au/news/pad/articles/2007/may/Love_hormone.html.

Uvnäs Moberg, K. 2003. *The Oxytocin Factor: Tapping the Hormone of Calm, Love, and Healing*. New York: Da Capo Press.

Uvnäs Moberg, K., A. M. Widström, E. Nissen, and H. Björvell. 1990. Personality traits in women 4 days postpartum and their correlation with plasma levels of oxytocin and prolactin. *Journal of Psychosomatic Obstetrics & Gynecology* 11 (4):261–73.

Verrelli, B., and S. Tishkoff. 2004. Signatures of selection and gene conversion associated with human color vision variation. *American Journal of Human Genetics* 75 (3):363–75.

Walker, B. R. 2007. Glucocorticoids and cardiovascular disease. *European Journal of Endocrinology* 157 (5):545–59.

Williams, J. R., K. C. Catania, and C. S. Carter. 1992. Development of partner preferences in female prairie voles (*Microtus ochrogaster*): The role of social and sexual experience. *Hormones and Behavior* 26 (3):339–49.

Wilson, C. L., W. S. Rholes, J. A. Simpson, and S. Tran. 2007. Labor, delivery, and early parenthood: An attachment theory perspective. *Personality and Social Psychology Bulletin* 33 (4):505–18.

Witt, D. M., C. S. Carter, and T. R. Insel. 1991. Oxytocin receptor binding in female prairie voles: Endogenous and exogenous oestradiol stimulation. *Journal of Neuroendocrinology* 3 (2):155–61.

Young, L. J., and Z. X. Wang. 2004. The neurobiology of pair bonding. *Nature Neuroscience* 7 (10):1048–54.

Zak, P. J. 2005. Trust: A temporary human attachment facilitated by oxytocin. *Behavioral and Brain Sciences* 28 (3):368–69.

Zak, P. J. 2007. Introduction: Moral markets—The critical role of values in the economy. *Free Enterprise: Values in Action Conference Series, 2005–2006*. Princeton, NJ: Princeton University Press.

Zak, P. J., K. Borja, W. T. Matzner, and R. Kurzban. 2005. The Neuroeconomics of distrust: Sex differences in behavior and physiology. *The American Economic Review* 95 (2):360–63.

Zak, P. J., R. Kurzban, and W. T. Matzner. 2005. Oxytocin is associated with human trustworthiness. *Hormones and Behavior* 48 (5):522–27.

Zak, P. J., A. A. Stanton, and S. Ahmadi. 2007. Oxytocin increases generosity in humans. *PLoS ONE* 2 (11): e1128. doi:10.1371/journal.pone.0001128.

Susan Kuchinskas is a journalist fascinated by what science can tell us about being human. She has published thousands of articles in *Time*, *Wired*, and many other publications. Kuchinskas is also a gardener, a welder, and a beekeeper, and lives in Berkeley, CA, with her mate, a dog, and a frog. Visit her oxytocin blog at www.hugthemonkey.com.

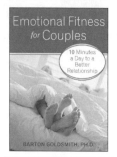

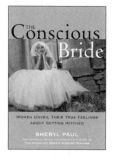
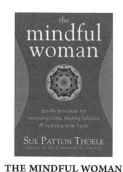